CHANEY
PLAYING FOR A LEGEND

CHANEY
PLAYING FOR A LEGEND

Donald Hunt
with
Special Commentary from
Aaron McKie and Eddie Jones

TRIUMPH
B O O K S
CHICAGO

Library of Congress Cataloging-in-Publication Data

Hunt, Donald, 1955–
    Chaney : playing for a legend / Donald Hunt ; with commentary by
Aaron McKie and Eddie Jones.
        p. cm.
    Includes index.
    ISBN 1-57243-580-1
        1. Chaney, John, 1932– 2. Basketball coaches—United States—Biography.
    3. Temple Owls (Basketball team)—History. I. McKie, Aaron. II. Jones, Eddie,
    1971– III. Title.

GV884.C53H86 2003
796.323'092—dc21
[B]
                                                                2003056418

This book is available in quantity at special discounts for your group or organization. For further information, contact:
    Triumph Books
    601 South LaSalle Street
    Suite 500
    Chicago, Illinois 60605
    (312) 939-3330
    Fax (312) 663-3557

Printed in the United States of America
ISBN: 1-57243-580-1
Interior design by Sue Knopf

Contents

Foreword

I remember watching Aaron McKie and Eddie Jones play against Duke. Temple coach John Chaney played five guys. I could see they were getting tired, and they wanted to come out of the game. You could see their tongues hanging out. But John wasn't going to take them off the floor. They had to continue playing. Keep on working.

John couldn't afford to sit them down. Even for a minute. Remember, he had only five guys. Usually, John finds a way to win, but not that day.

It's not easy playing for him. You have to be intelligent to play on his team. It's a different level of intelligence. John's players hold the ball for the good shot. They work the ball around the court about five or six times before they take a shot. It's one thing to watch Princeton, a paramount academic institution, play that way. People are used to watching their style of play. John's players learn patience and perseverance.

On the recruiting side, we are not Duke. We are not Syracuse. We are not UCLA. We are not even St. John's. If you look at Temple's campus, you don't hear a church bell as you walk to class. You don't hear the school fight song. You've got the Broad Street Subway, cement, and tar. That's it.

Academically, we don't demand 1,400 on the SAT. Nor is our price $50,000. We have to recruit a kid who is a special person. This player is going to have to get up at 5:30 in the morning to go to practice. He's going to play for a man who doesn't have cuteness or puppy stories to tell. You're not going to get that from him.

All you have to do is look at his face. You see that glazed look. That's what a kid is going to see for four years. That face tells you a lot about your future. It says things are going to be rough.

While John is tough, he's also caring. He's going to holler at times, but he's going to give you discipline, guidance, and direction. These things are going to help you down the road. Much of what he tells you is preventative. In the motto of Fat Albert, "If you pay attention, you just might learn something."

Listening is important. If you listen to Aaron, Eddie, and some of the others who have played for John, they will tell you how he's a father figure to them. Well, they should look at him as a friend.

Kids usually listen to their fathers. But after a while they have a tendency to not listen as well as they should. They'll listen more to a friend. As a friend, John has told these kids where to go, what to wear, and what to do for years. And they've listened very well through all the yelling and screaming they've had to hear from him.

His players are too young to know how tough John really is. He would not be a good Jesus. I remember giving Sonny Hill some money to start Dr. Cosby's Over-40 Liniment League. If you don't know what liniment is, it's ointment for old folks. We used to put that on to ease the pain in our muscles.

The league lasted four games. You heard me right—four games. Chaney was the worst behaved player. If the referee called a foul on him, he would take the ball from the official. Now, John knew he wasn't allowed to do that.

John knows a lot of things. He may get upset, but he knows what he's doing. He speaks very loudly. Then again, John has a message. Whatever he's saying, the kids listen and come back to practice the next day. They even call him for advice after college. Believe it or not, I've called him for advice about my wife.

John's success is measured in several ways. He doesn't need a lot of talent. He would take some of his worst teams to the NCAA Tournament. He could win with less talent better than anybody I know. What keeps him going is the relationship with his players. I think he enjoys talking to them as much as they enjoy listening to him. Why? It's very simple. He cares about the kids.

—Bill Cosby

Foreword

When I look at Aaron McKie and Eddie Jones, I see two young men who have accomplished so much despite some very difficult circumstances. Eddie grew up poor in a rural community in Pompano Beach, Florida. His father died when he was in high school. It was such a devastating loss, Eddie thought about leaving school and giving up on life. Fortunately, he listened to his mother and stayed in school.

Things weren't easy for Aaron, either. His father passed away when he was eight years old. After that, Aaron stayed briefly with a sister who had children of her own. At 14, he moved in with an elderly aunt in a tough North Philadelphia neighborhood about five blocks away from the Temple campus.

If there were ever two kids who could have thrown in the towel, it was Aaron and Eddie. The amazing thing about them is they really wanted to go to Temple. We couldn't give them scholarships because of the NCAA's Proposition 48 policy. Their high school grades were fine, but they didn't have the required SAT scores.

So, they had to take out huge loans just to go to Temple. And these kids came from families who didn't have any money. They were thousands of dollars in debt before they played a minute of college basketball. They didn't deserve to be punished, but that is exactly what happened to them. It was a tough pill to swallow. To their credit, Aaron and Eddie never complained, which says a lot about their character.

They should be revered for what they accomplished at Temple. They always went to class. They never missed a tutoring session. They always got to practice on time.

You should reward people for hard work. That's what we did one summer. Aaron was picked to play for Team USA. Eddie was selected to play for the USA Under-22 Team in the World University Games. I wouldn't let a lot of our kids play for all-star teams in the summer. They had to go to summer school. But I spoke to their academic counselors, and they told me Aaron and Eddie could miss one summer session.

So, I decided to let them go. It was a tribute not only to them, but to Temple basketball, too. I appreciated that they came to me in the very beginning. As soon as they heard about the opportunity, Aaron and Eddie said, "Coach, can we go?" That really says something about them. They appreciate the things that have been done for them.

Aaron and Eddie are role models for a lot of kids coming up. You look at where they've come from and where they are right now and it sends a message to youngsters: "I can make it, too."

When Aaron and Eddie came to Temple in 1991, we didn't know how good they were going to be. We knew Aaron had been well coached at Simon Gratz High School by Bill Ellerbee, who is on our staff now. We knew Eddie had a lot of talent, but we weren't sure how quickly he would be able to adjust to our style of play.

Everything turned out well for them. They went to NCAA Tournaments all three years they were eligible to play for us.

Each was Atlantic 10 Player of the Year, and they received a lot of accolades across the country. They both became NBA first-round picks. Aaron and Eddie have been in the NBA for eight years now. They've made a lot of money. They're doing very well.

As a coach, I've had plenty of kids go to the NBA, but that's not important to me. I'm just happy we were able to give them a chance to improve their lives. Now they can go out and help others who didn't have the same opportunities they did. Aaron and Eddie have established the John Chaney Sr. Endowed Scholarship Fund to help many youngsters receive a quality education. They have made me extremely proud because they are not just good basketball players, but great people, too.

—*John Chaney*

Preface

Aaron McKie and Eddie Jones are two of my favorite people, so I wanted this book to be something special. And it is.

Aaron and Eddie trusted me enough to tell me about the tough times in their lives, as well as the thrilling successes. They don't pretend that their stories prove that any underprivileged kid in America can go to college and get a great job. They tell about the good people who helped them overcome major obstacles.

John Chaney, of course, had a major influence on their lives and careers after others—credited throughout this book—put them in position to get an opportunity. Aaron and Eddie are among the Simon Gratz High, Cheyney State, and Temple alumni using the Chaneysian (Reggie Bryant's word) teachings to arrive earlier, work harder, show and earn respect, stay honest and loyal, avoid trouble and scandal, do the little things right, and help and encourage other people.

Former Temple players Mark Macon, Donald Hodge, and Rick Brunson have made the NBA, Mark Karcher is playing overseas, and Kevin Lyde is playing for the Greenville Groove (National Basketball Development League). I don't know any other coach who could have prepared Tim Perry, Ramon Rivas,

Duane Causwell, Nate Blackwell, Mark Strickland, Terence Stansbury, William Cunningham, Aaron, and Eddie—all former Temple players—for the NBA.

I met Aaron when he played for the Bill Cosby Future League team that's now sponsored by Eddie; he later played for the Hank Gathers College League team that's also sponsored by Eddie. Aaron was a husky kid who wasn't at all quick, but he tried hard. He told me he was used to overpowering kids his own age, but in the Cosby League he was getting his shots smacked back off his face. By mid-July he was shooting jump shots and making some. It was obvious that he had shot a lot of them between games.

Aaron thrived with the Medics (sponsored for 33 years by Dr. Myron Rodos) in the Sonny Hill League's Wilt Chamberlain High School Division. Medics coach John Hardnett has been Aaron's mentor through the best and worst times. The smartest thing Eddie ever did, career-wise, was become Aaron's friend and latch on to his support group. Eddie was lucky that Aaron was the kind of good person whom people want to help. Eddie had to be of good character or Aaron wouldn't have brought him to Hardnett.

The summer before Aaron entered Temple, I showed him the pages in Steve Wartenberg's excellent book about Chaney, *Winning Is an Attitude*, in which Chaney said he'd coach four more years because Aaron was a wonderful young man who had gone through hard times so well that he wanted to see Aaron graduate, get a good job, marry a good woman, and enjoy a good family life. "Wow!" Aaron said. "He wants all that for me? I don't want to disappoint him and everyone else who has helped me. I am going to work hard." Chaney never said he hoped Aaron McKie would be Atlantic 10 Player of the Year or a first-round NBA pick with a guaranteed six-year contract.

McKie's chances at stardom seemed limited. He didn't run or jump very well, and his shot came and went. His main assets were his good intentions, his willingness to be coached, and an incredible work ethic fueled by insecurity caused by life experiences.

Eddie was the opposite. He was highly athletic and had some skills. He just was skinny and weak, with fragile ankles. His outside shooting and deft ball handling came along. His one great Owl season was his senior year.

McKie and Jones were Proposition 48 victims and had to sit out their first year.

I remember Essie "Coach" Davis, Temple basketball secretary since Harry Litwack's final years in the new McGonigle, asking me if Aaron was as polite, sincere, and appreciative as he seemed, or one more slick kid. She would ask the same of Lynard Stewart. They were Medics, as was her own son, Jonathon Craig-Davis. But so was slick agent Mik Kilgore.

Of Jones, coach Davis said, "We've had some skinny kids here [such as Dr. Ed Coe, Nate Blackwell, Mark Davis, and Darrin Pearsall], but I saw Eddie and said to myself, 'Oh, you poor child.'"

Aaron's best friend and roommate, Jonathan Haynes, left Temple after not playing at Iowa and Villanova—although Chaney kept him on scholarship a second semester before Nova accepted him. Eddie stayed in his room for weeks, but then he heard how much basketball Aaron was playing in Pearson Hall. Eddie started joining Aaron. It was difficult to be one of the only Prop guys, especially for someone far from home.

I saw Aaron after a Sunday Temple practice. He didn't introduce the tall, skinny kid with him, but I figured it must have been this Eddie Jones. Young Mr. Jones wasn't ready to be introduced to Philadelphia basketball, but he stayed close to Aaron and learned who was who.

Eddie led his team of students to the Temple intramural league championship. Aaron said he himself had averaged 43 points for the Temple police team, but he was disgusted with the team's poor performance. A young policeman blamed himself: "I was the point guard. When I got assigned the night shift, Aaron was left with slow, old married men with bad feet. We all loved Aaron."

The summer of 1990, Aaron had led the precollege Pep Boys over all of the college guys in the Hank Gathers League. Now he was afraid that every eligible varsity player in America had caught up and passed him. He worked hard to prepare for the College League and got Eddie to work with him.

I drafted Aaron (when a team has no coach at the meeting, surrogates are appointed by Hardnett) with the final pick in the first round of the College League draft. Ike Cahoe, one of Donald Hunt's Lincoln U. pals and father of former Coppin State hero Antoine Brockington, drafted Eddie midway in the second round. Years later, Cahoe would see Eddie embarrass Shawn Bradley and the Philadelphia 76ers, win a halftime shooting contest, and go to the NBA All-Star Game in Phoenix.

Eddie scored 35 points in his College League debut at St. Joseph's Alumni Memorial Fieldhouse. Rival Bernard Blunt said aloud, "Who is that?" In subsequent Temple–St. Joseph's games, Blunt would continually shove Jones toward the cheerleaders behind the baseline. To Eddie's credit, he kept coming back to the court. When Eddie staggered backward or fell, he often got fouls called in his favor. Aaron, on the other hand, simply refused to be budged—Bernard knew he was no pushover.

The late Henry Smith, a former St. Joseph's rebounding champion, coached the Hank Gathers College League blackshirt team. He said he didn't want to help any Temple or Villanova players, but he couldn't help loving Aaron.

Henry was succeeded by best friend Rodney Wescott, who drafted gunners and at-risk personalities. Kareem Townes' South Philadelphia fans called Aaron names and shouted for him not to shoot. As a Medic, Aaron had great games against South Philadelphia every time the loud people showed up. When Townes was away one week, Gene Lett filled in and Aaron averaged 42 points. Gene now works as Aaron's administrative assistant. Loyal and smart.

McKie and Jones work out every summer with other pros and with Temple players. They usually play one another because Aaron wants to be tested by someone taller and quicker and Eddie needs to be challenged by someone stronger.

Said Eddie, "He feels he has to work harder than everyone else in the world or he is cheating himself and everyone who ever helped him. Me? I do enough."

Jones is correct. Aaron has a workhorse body and mentality, although overwork, tendinitis, and other strains periodically cause his body to go on strike and demand a vacation. Eddie is a thoroughbred who has gotten stronger. Eddie spent many hours in Temple's training room. Aaron wouldn't admit to pain until a trainer found his socks were bloody. I didn't see Aaron dunk until his senior year at Temple. He surprised everyone with a left-handed dunk for the 76ers in 1999.

Eddie loves to dunk, especially in the summer, without an audience.

When William Cunningham was a Temple senior-to-be, he said, "Coach said we'd better not hurt the millionaires, but he didn't tell the millionaires not to hurt us. Eddie loves to dunk on tall people, and I'm the biggest here. I just catch him in midair and put him down gently."

McKie got quicker and was Atlantic 10 Player of the Year as a junior in 1993. Jones got stronger and took that honor the following season. In August before their senior season, each scored over 40 in the Hank Gathers College League championship game. This time, Aaron won. They were co-MVPs.

I didn't enjoy Temple games—Aaron would miss shots and I'd think of the Continental Basketball Association's Sioux Falls Skyforce team—but I learned a lot at Temple's Saturday or Sunday practices. I remember Chaney yelling at Aaron for passing to bad-hands big men Derrick Battie (his roommate) and William Cunningham. Battie would become pass-worthy the following year.

I suspected Chaney just wanted the big guys to know Aaron wasn't to blame for not passing to them. Many Owl big men have become go-to guys after years of no-go. They have to earn it.

Aaron wants people to like him. He tries to help people feel better about themselves. Eddie, never as insecure, has become more outgoing, at least in comfortable surroundings. He wants respect. He is helping people through his Eddie Jones Foundation. With Aaron, giving starts with family, even to those who didn't help when he was desperate. Eddie has a good memory and a short list.

I once saw Eddie, watching a Sonny Hill League game, talking with a high school coach who wanted to arrange a preseason game for his team. I later asked the coach why he was trying to get a game with the Lakers through Eddie Jones. The coach said, "You mean that wasn't Kobe Bryant [then a Lower Merion High School junior] I was talking to? No wonder he had a strange look." Eddie didn't take offense or embarrass the coach. He seems to be in a great mood every time he returns to Temple.

NBA draft night in 1994 was typically different for Eddie and Aaron. Eddie had a great workout with the Lakers ("Michael Cooper played me and I didn't miss a shot until Jerry West said, 'That's enough'"). West said he'd make Jones the Lakers' first lottery pick, and he did. Willis Reed told McKie he'd be the Nets' first-rounder, so Aaron was shocked ("Is this happening to me again?") when David Stern announced the Nets' selection of Yinka Dare, who'd been shut out by William Cunningham in an Atlantic 10 tourney rout.

Geoff Petrie, former Charles Baker League and NBA Rookie of the Year, selected Aaron for Portland, as far from home as possible. Aaron, however, was comfortable with coach P. J. Carlesimo, for whom Aaron had played on a USA Basketball team one summer. P. J. had Aaron backing up Billy McCaffrey of Vanderbilt, a team Temple had crushed in the NCAA tourney the previous season.

Eddie moved from small forward (third guard in Chaney's system) to shooting guard in L.A. and soon earned a starting spot. He became the first Chaney disciple to make the NBA All-Star Game, doing so twice.

Aaron was a reserve on a solid, old Portland team, soon to become a young and crazy team as new GM Bob Whitsitt collected lottery picks who'd bad-acted their way off other franchises. We advised Aaron to hook up with Charles "Buck" Williams, a responsible Sonny Hill League alumnus, but Buck soon left for New York. Aaron became a starter for Portland after Clyde Drexler went to Houston, but the Trail Blazers dealt for J. R. Rider from the Minnesota Timberwolves and Aaron was dealt to Detroit for Stacey Augmon. His biggest game for the Pistons came when he filled in at small forward for Grant Hill.

Larry Brown, first-year 76ers coach, sent North Carolina favorites Jerry Stackhouse and Eric Montross to Detroit for McKie and Theo Ratliff, popular in Philadelphia ever since agent Joel Bell sent him to the John Hardnett–Fred Douglas workouts before the NBA Draft. Aaron and Theo made the 76ers much stronger on defense. Theo now plays for the Atlanta Hawks.

Aaron's best statistic is the plus-minus. The Sixers just do better when he is in the game. He looks to shoot only when he is open and the team has the floor balanced, so big men are in place to rebound his misses and the team can get back on defense. He doesn't foul jump shooters, but he makes them hurry and change shots.

Eddie made a lot of showy dunks, often off steals, for the Lakers, and he managed to stay out of the way. When the Lakers finally traded him and Elden Campbell to Charlotte for Glen Rice and J. R. Reid, they weakened themselves at three positions on defense. The trade was opposed by scores of Lakers fans and such observers as Wilt Chamberlain, Guy Rodgers, and even Wayne Gretzky.

Jerry West, who nearly retired because he was sick of knuckle-heads, loved Eddie's demeanor and said it was representative of Temple's class. No matter how spectacular the play, Eddie didn't celebrate, taunt, or forget to play defense. As for Aaron, Larry Brown played him in clutch situations because Brown could count on him to play the game the right way.

Temple's NBA guys seem to know what not to do and where not to go and whom to avoid.

Allen Iverson brought his posse to Philadelphia from Hampton, Virginia. Aaron brought Craig "Bus" White to Portland. A former Lafayette College captain, Craig used to help Medics with rebounding, manners, grammar, vocabulary, and work ethic. John Hardnett once said Mik Kilgore was the only Public League to qualify for an NCAA scholarship in 1988 because his SAT score gained 10 points every hour he spent with Craig. Randy Woods once told me he was helping his image by standing next to Craig White.

I met Chaney when he was coaching Kent's Taverneers to a fifth straight Charles Baker League championship. He made veterans Hal Greer and Chet Walker do more for him than they did in the NBA, where they had Wilt Chamberlain, Wali Jones, and Luke Jackson for major roles.

Chaney has been very protective of image—at Simon Gratz, at Cheyney, and especially at Temple—and has avoided several high-maintenance talents. He wants his players to present themselves as the kind of people someone would like to hire and to represent their school as a quality institution people would be proud to attend. He wants to prove that underprivileged kids can show dignity and succeed academically if given a chance.

Chaney is strongly opposed to NCAA keep-out rules because he knows that he and so many good people that he's met would have been denied opportunity under the current exclusionary rules. He wasn't given college prep courses at Ben Franklin High and had a tryout only at Bethune-Cookman, now Division I.

At Gratz, he made sure every player had college prep courses. He used extraordinary measures to get players into colleges. His players addressed adults formally.

He and other Gratz teachers started a free breakfast program, now funded throughout the city of Philadelphia. Chaney found he could feed the multitudes with a 29¢ box of grits.

He called his players at home every night, making sure they were doing homework instead of playing around.

He has said high school coaches shouldn't be expected to do things not in the job description, but the system should do more, sooner.

"If a kid can't hardly read in the 12th grade," he said at a Sportsters Club meeting, "he probably couldn't hardly read in the second grade. Spend what it takes to make classes smaller and emphasize reading in the early grades and we'll have a lot less trouble."

At Cheyney, he got faculty volunteers to help his Wolves. Many who would have been excluded by today's Division II Prop 64 graduated. When he got the job, several Cheyney alums in the Baker League were told, "You got out in time. The party is over."

Chaney's 1978 Wolves—with Sonny Hill Leaguers Milton Colston, Dana Clark, Roger Leysath, and Charles Murphy among the mainstays—won an NCAA Division II championship.

Chaney and Sonny Hill have had a lasting effect on Philadelphia basketball. Sonny Hill Leaguers tend to do well at every college level because they are accustomed to playing halfcourt basketball and dealing with traps and weakside help. Playing in air conditioning gets kids used to making full-speed decisions and moves. Kids who get used to lax defense and easy baskets in soft, warm summer leagues aren't as ready for college basketball.

The main thing about Chaney's teaching style is that people remember what he says. Daryl "Silky Smooth" Oliver told me that former Cheyney coach Keith Johnson had told the team: "If you really must have a girlfriend, find someone ugly who is an A student and a good typist." Johnson got that from Chaney, and Chaney brought it to Temple, where he found it harder to control social situations. Terence Stansbury said, "I looked and I couldn't find an ugly girl on this campus. They must all go to Cheyney."

Charlie Rayne played for Milt Colston and the Camille Cosby team in the Sonny Hill College League before playing for Chaney at Temple. "Coach Chaney uses the exact same words as Milt, and Milt really knows basketball. They both told a story about an old mule and a young mule."

The next summer, Chaney walked onto the McGonigle court and kissed Rayne for playing great defense, with his repaired knee, against Albert "Truck" Butts. Chaney returned to his familiar seat in the corner and told me, "I never kissed Keith Johnson and told him how much I appreciated him. I'm going to go home and tell my son John I love him and I'm proud of him. I have to get better."

I told Keith Johnson, and he said, "Coach fed me. He didn't have to kiss me." Rayne proudly says, "I am the first Temple player coach Chaney kissed." But hardly the last.

When Chaney was coach at Simon Gratz, he placed a chair behind one basket and ordered junior Joe Anderson, his star player, to watch only Tom "Trooper" Washington, of Gaddie Real Estate and ABA title teams.

"I did watch just Trooper," Anderson said, "and I learned how to rebound better, move my feet, set picks, and do all the little things to help his team win. The next summer, before Temple, I watched Frank 'Watusi' Card and saw how he makes the women go 'Woooo.' And I liked that."

Dr. Marcus Foster brought Chaney to Gratz in 1966 as the second black basketball head coach in Public League history, replacing the first, John Glenn, who was promoted to vice principal. Gratz, mostly a girls school because Franklin and Edison were all-boys, had been a doormat. With some recruiting and people wanting sons to play for Chaney, the Bulldogs became major winners.

Chaney left Gratz for Cheyney in 1972 partly because the public schools were headed for a long strike. During the strike, Sonny Hill organized a Sonny Hill Winter League. Tee Shields coached a Gratz team that had been floundering in December to the championship, with Joe Gore, Larry Pittman, Marvin Brown, and Greg Pouncy. Many of them had played for Chaney on Gratz's JV soccer team, which hardly ever allowed a goal.

Chaney in 1999 was voted Philadelphia's best college coach of all time in a *Daily News* poll. Back in 1982, people at the *Daily News, Inquirer*, WCAU-TV, and WIP-AM suggested that Temple president Peter Liacouras was about to hire a little-known Division II black coach just to help himself politically. I wrote in the *Philadelphia Tribune* that if Chaney had been unavailable (he thought he had the Seton Hall job, only to be passed over for P. J. Carlesimo), the choice would have been Jim Maloney, who was more Irish-Catholic than Don Casey, who rejected an associate athletic director job in favor of the Chicago Bulls staff and a long NBA career.

Chaney felt blessed to inherit two of his best friends, Maloney and Jay Norman, from Casey's staff. Chaney had coached man-to-man in the Eastern League and Baker League as well as at William Sayre Junior High and Simon Gratz. At Cheyney, he had tall men who committed reaching fouls. He turned to Maloney for matchup zone lessons and to Norman for tips on coaching big men.

John and Jim enjoyed recruiting Darby-Colwyn's Kevin Clifton and sharing rides, dinners, and game peanuts. Maloney got Clifton with a Temple scholarship, but Kevin became the first Owl to play four seasons for Chaney. His "Jack in the Box" pass to Terence Stansbury started the 18-game run over Penn. Graduated, good job, wife and kids.

At first, Chaney found fault with tutoring director Jon Cohen, a nice man who sympathized with problems of the disadvantaged. "I want the kids to be afraid of getting their heads driven through the wall if they miss class or don't turn in a paper or flunk tests," Chaney said. Cohen, however, found Temple hoopsters came to tutoring with a much more serious attitude than ever before. And head knocking was not necessary.

Because Granger Hall had some afternoon classes, Chaney scheduled practices at 6:00 A.M. those days. He later went to 5:30 A.M. practices on weekdays, assuring that players finished basketball early, ate breakfast, went to every class with a free mind, then did homework, went to tutoring, and enjoyed social life while most of NCAA basketball was practicing. Temple schedules most road games on weekends, limiting the number of classes missed.

"We've had a lot of players miss class," Essie "Coach" Davis has said. "I can't remember the last player who did it twice."

One summer, Chaney withheld permission for Aaron and Eddie to play in the Hank Gathers College League until they got better grades in summer school. When I saw Eddie and didn't see Aaron several times, I worried about him. He finally showed up, embarrassed. I expected Aaron to struggle with biology, but he also got a C in weightlifting. "I lifted better than anyone else," Aaron said, "but she said I didn't participate enough in discussions. I didn't think it was much to talk about."

Aaron was grateful for his tutors—especially Kym Norsworthy—for helping him catch up.

Aaron majored in social work, Eddie in sports administration. They didn't need the stuff they didn't know on the SAT. And few of the hundreds of kids who cheated on the SAT and

ACT—documented in the book *Raw Recruits* and in *Sports Illustrated*—got as much out of their college experience.

When Chaney bought a satellite dish for his bedroom, his wife, Jeanne, told him, "I understand that Temple could play North Carolina or UCLA or Kansas or UNLV in the tournament. Temple will not play the San Antonio Spurs. Go to sleep."

Chaney now has several reasons to watch NBA games all over. When the calls come, he has something to say. When Duane Causwell complained that Dick Motta had him playing far from the basket and trying to pass into little guys, Chaney said, "You know and I know that you don't belong in the NBA. Give them back the money and come back to school." Causwell, who said he'd never been coached before Temple, played more than a decade in the NBA. The NBA Owls can expect some tough love, advice, and laughs when they call.

Philadelphia's Comcast Sportsnet invited Eddie, Aaron, Rick Brunson, and Mark Macon to explain why they keep returning to Temple and Chaney.

"Our last game," Eddie said, "we lost to Indiana in the NCAA. Coach got outcoached by Bobby Knight." He laughed. "Bobby Knight outcoached Coach."

Chaney laughed. Eddie has earned the right to make a little joke.

Dean Demopoulos, who discovered Eddie and pushed for Aaron, is Chaney's choice as his successor, but not for a while. I met Dean in 1982, when he was a graduate student charting Temple practices from the upstairs stands and working as a bouncer. At this writing, Demopoulos is a Seattle SuperSonics assistant.

Chaney has had a graduate student charting Temple on TV shows and on radio. He had Jim Maloney doing a half-hour Temple pregame show on radio.

When Chaney coached at Cheyney, he and Maloney left a Sonny Hill League game and disappeared for 36 minutes.

"I had a terrific new play," Chaney said. "We went back to the basketball office and I put it on the board. Right away, Maloney showed me how to destroy my play. I said I was going to use this play because I wouldn't coach against people like him.

"I said, 'Maloney, if I ever get a Division I job, I want you to come along, because you are incredible. You can even wear the white hat and make intelligent explanations after we win the same simple way.'"

If selected, Demopoulos would inherit more than Chaney did. At Chaney's introductory press conference, sportswriters questioned how Chaney would ever bring good players to North Broad Street. The Associated Press scoffed at the notion that Chaney would bring big-name opponents to Philadelphia.

Chaney said he had won before without cheating and would do so again. He said he'd schedule only Division I teams and that Temple was moving from the East Coast Conference to the stronger Atlantic 10. He said Granger Hall was one of the best players in America.

Well, there have been no scandals. He has sent more players to the NBA than any Philadelphia coach. Temple had had no NCAA tourney wins since 1958. But since Terence Stansbury's bomb shocked St. John's in 1984, the Owls have averaged better than one NCAA win per year. The Owls have dominated Big Five play and become a regular on national TV.

The ten thousand–seat Liacouras Center makes a statement for Chaney, Temple, and North Philadelphia. Aaron,

Eddie, and other Chaney protégés make a statement every time they represent their coach, their school, and their own families and neighborhoods with hard work and dignity.

Chaney and Tom Gola were honored by the William Markward Basketball Club in 1951 as the best senior players in the Philadelphia Public and Catholic Leagues. As guest speaker at Wednesday luncheons in which the Markward honors high school seniors, Chaney has told how I sent him his first Cheyney recruit, a kid who was blind in one eye and had a bullet in him too dangerous to remove.

Frank Kravitz, hired by Temple to keep people out of the new McGonigle Hall, got permission to start a Temple Community League in old South Hall's third floor gym. I saw McKinley "Killer" Walker grabbing powerful rebounds and found he was an Edison High senior with no college commitment. I sent Chaney a note on McKinley and another kid. Chaney called me and said he'd been working with an Edison counselor to get McKinley into Cheyney despite his poor attendance. (The bullet had convinced Walker that it was not safe to go to school.)

McKinley did a lot of catching up academically before he played for Cheyney. As a senior, he asked Chaney if he could quit the team so he could get the credits he needed to graduate. With Andrew Fields and Roger Leysath up front, the Wolves won the 1978 NCAA Division II title without Walker.

"When I went to McKinley's home," Chaney said, "I saw his mother with a bunch of little girls, washing a big load of clothes. When I said I wanted McKinley to come to Cheyney, his mother was thrilled. She had no idea he could go to college. We found out about the bad eye when he kept turning his head to find the ball. He had to go back to have the bullet checked. He played hard and everyone loved him. And he graduated.

"The best thing is that those little sisters of his all went to college and graduated. Marcus Foster used to say that if you give one young person an opportunity and help that youngster succeed, you will give hope and direction to that family for generations to come."

Edward Geiger was 6'9", but he never played for Murrell Dobbins Tech and arrived at the Sonny Hill League as a terribly raw talent.

"His first year at Cheyney," Chaney said, "we just had him throw the ball against a wall and catch it. The wall usually won."

Geiger developed into a center who would play pro ball in Argentina. He was sent there by Haverford High soccer coach George Severini, who later would give Chaney Pepe Sanchez.

In August 1982, Essie "Coach" Davis said, "This tall character keeps coming into the office and saying, 'Y'all stole my coach. John Chaney is a great man and he saved my life. You treat him right or you will answer to me.' I wanted to punch him in his knee!"

Geiger graduated and became a teacher. He offers unsolicited messages about values and work ethic to young hoopsters. Like so many, he passes on the Chaneysian philosophy.

Chaney perhaps owes his career to the late Sam Browne, his Ben Franklin High coach, who went to a construction site and pleaded with stepfather Sylvester Chaney to allow John to try college.

"When I went to see Sam in the hospital," Chaney said, "they told me that only relatives were permitted to see him. I said, 'He is my Jewish father.' Sam Browne was a great man and a great [English] teacher. He wasn't a great coach because he got emotional during games, he wanted so much for us to succeed."

Before Philadelphia was belatedly wired for cable, I bought a satellite dish from Walter Byrd, a Temple alum who starred in the Baker League and Eastern League. I often invited John Hardnett, who brought some Medics and his friend James "Mr. Class" Flint Sr. Three of those kids made it to the NBA: Doug Overton, Larry Stewart, and Aaron. Hardnett was transforming Overton into a point guard. To boost his assertiveness, he had Doug call in the prehalftime order to New Station Pizza. ("Now listen up. . . . Read that back. . . . We'll be there in five minutes.") I can't recall Aaron saying anything but "thank you, Mr. Rogul."

I want to thank Mr. McKie (and Mr. Jones) for helping me through some difficult times by providing thrills and satisfaction. And becoming responsible, helpful adults.

And thank you, Donald, for the work it took to put this book together.

—Herm Rogul

Editor's Note: Herm Rogul, who had 6,234 sports bylines in the old *Philadelphia Bulletin* and 1,110 in the *Philadelphia Tribune*, now writes for the *News* of Delaware County.

Acknowledgments

During my college days at Lincoln University, my school used to play Cheyney State. The head coach of Cheyney State was John Chaney. Lincoln and Cheyney had one of the greatest rivalries in the country among historically black colleges and universities. Cheyney had one of the best college basketball programs in the country. Chaney's teams used to beat Lincoln regularly. And we had some pretty good teams, too. I attended Lincoln from 1973 to '77. I could see way back then that Chaney was bound for greatness. Actually, he had already achieved national recognition among small colleges across the nation. In 1978 he led Cheyney State to an NCAA Division II championship. Fortunately, Dr. Peter Liacouras, Temple president, recognized his outstanding work and hired him to coach the Owls in 1982.

I was really happy for him. I knew Chaney had the knowledge and experience to build the Temple basketball program into a national power. In 2001 he was inducted into the Naismith Basketball Hall of Fame. As I wrote in my book, *The Philadelphia Big 5*, I was pleased that Kevin Clifton had a chance to play for Chaney. Kevin and I grew up in Darby, Pennsylvania. I knew Chaney was recruiting him when he was still coaching at Cheyney. I remember telling everybody how fortunate Kevin was to play for Chaney. Kevin wasn't a big star with the Owls. However, he was one of many players who Chaney has coached over his last 21 years at Temple.

Two of Chaney's most notable players are Aaron McKie and Eddie Jones. Both players had to sit out their freshman seasons because of NCAA Proposition 42, which prevented students with either a sub 2.000 grade-point average or a sub 700 SAT score from receiving financial aid. (Prop 42 has since been rescinded.) But Aaron and Eddie bounced back to perform extremely well on and off the court. It's not easy coaching college basketball players these days. The majority of them were stars on their high school teams. Most of them feel they're going to be All-Americans and eventually NBA players. Aaron and Eddie weren't spoiled like most kids today. They didn't come to Temple with attitudes and preconceived notions of stardom. They were just happy to be in school. Aaron and Eddie made coaching very enjoyable for Chaney.

"Aaron and Eddie never gave me any trouble," Chaney said. "It was a pleasure coaching them. They did everything I asked them to do. They went to class and did all the things they needed to do. They both had great playing careers. I was really happy to see them both become first-round draft picks and go to the NBA. That was special for me. But what's more important is that they can reach back and help others. Aaron and Eddie always call to let me know how things are going for them. They stop around during the summer to play with some of the kids. This shows me that they care. If you see one, you usually see the other."

Aaron and Eddie met each other on the basketball court. They were playing pickup ball with some of the players at Temple's McGonigle Hall. That's where the relationship began.

Aaron and Eddie did a lot of things together. They took classes together. They went out to eat together. They studied together. They went to games together. They were like peanut butter and jelly. Aaron and Eddie are still good friends today.

Aaron and Eddie reflect the kind of players who have played for Chaney. They don't have big egos. They're fundamentally sound. They don't cause any problems off the court.

"You can tell Eddie played for coach Chaney," said Kobe Bryant, Jones' former Los Angeles Lakers teammate. "He does all the little things like hustling, playing good defense, and hitting the open man. I learned a lot from playing with him."

Larry Brown, former Philadelphia 76ers coach now coaching the Detroit Pistons, has known Chaney for a long time. He faced him during his coaching days at Kansas. Aaron has played five seasons for Brown.

"I've known John Chaney for many years," Brown said. "He's more than a basketball coach to his kids. He teaches them good values and standards. I can see them in Aaron. I can see it in the way he plays on the court. I can see it in the way he carries himself in public. We're very fortunate to have a player like him."

Aaron and Eddie have really benefited from playing for Chaney. This book clearly illustrates that in so many ways.

"For all the things he's done for me," Eddie said, "I could never repay him." Said McKie: "I'm really lucky to have someone like coach Chaney be a part of my life."

Writing this book with two of Temple's greatest players, Aaron McKie and Eddie Jones, was truly enlightening. I spent a lot of time interviewing them during a hectic NBA season. At times, I was up as late as 2:00 A.M. talking to Aaron and Eddie on the phone. I couldn't have written this book without their cooperation. I also had a lot of help from several people.

First, I would like to thank John Chaney for his support. Aaron and Eddie didn't want to do the book without his approval. Secondly, I want to thank John Hardnett, Herm Rogul, Bill Ellerbee, James "Bruiser" Flint, Rick Brunson, Gene Lett, Mark Macon, Shawn Pastor (editor of the *Owl Scoop*), Dr. Peter J. Liacouras (former Temple president), Doug Gordon (of P. M. Gordon Associates), and Ms. Essie Davis (coach Chaney's secretary). Al Shrier, Brian Kirschner, Chet Zukowski, and Carlos Bater provided a great deal of assistance from Temple's sports information department (Kirschner currently works for the Philadelphia 76ers media relations department). Thirdly, Joe Amato of NBA Photos, Temple photographer Zohrab Kazanjian, and photographer Rodney Adams did a great job of providing photos for the book. Thanks also to the James A. Naismith Basketball Hall of Fame.

I would also like to thank Barnett Wright, former *Philadelphia Tribune* associate managing editor, Mike Kern, *Philadelphia Daily News* sportswriter, and Mike Jensen, *Philadelphia Inquirer* sportswriter, for their encouragement.

Lastly, I would like to thank my wife, Pat, who assisted me with the book; my son, Donald Richard Brown Hunt; and my daughter, Arielle Elizabeth Alexandria, for all their patience and understanding during the time I was writing the book.

Introduction

BIOGRAPHY OF A LEGEND

John Chaney has never been one to heap praise on himself. Chaney has spent most of his life paving the way for others. He's a man who has excelled in many areas, such as life lessons, education, and basketball. If you listen to him talk, you'll learn quite a bit in just one conversation. He can be enlightening, serious, and entertaining.

Nate Blackwell was Chaney's first recruit at Temple. Blackwell was an All–Public League basketball star at South Philadelphia High School. Blackwell received plenty of calls from major college basketball coaches. But the first call came from Chaney.

"Coach Chaney called me right away," Blackwell said. "It was the first day coaches were allowed to contact players. There were a lot of people who called after him, but coach Chaney was definitely the first. That made a big impression on me. He hadn't been at Temple that long. He really wanted me to be a part of something special."

Blackwell finished his career (1984–87) as the Owls' all-time leader in games played, second in career assists, and third in career scoring. He was a unanimous choice as the Atlantic 10 Conference Player of the Year following his senior year.

He also led the Owls to four consecutive NCAA Tournaments. Undoubtedly, Blackwell helped Chaney put Temple basketball on the map.

These years, he said, have great significance now that Chaney has been inducted into the Naismith Basketball Hall of Fame (in 2001).

"I'm just happy to be a part of his success," said Blackwell, former assistant coach under Chaney. "Coach Chaney did a tremendous job of building the program. We played our games at McGonigle Hall. Now, we play at the Liacouras Center. We went from a four thousand–seat facility to a ten thousand–seat arena. We're playing on national television. He's responsible for that. We won a lot of games to put him in this position. But coach Chaney guided us to another level."

Chaney has touched a number of people, most notably the players he's coached over the years. Every summer former Temple players such as Aaron McKie, Eddie Jones, Rick Brunson, Derrick Battie, Tim Perry, Marc Jackson, and others come back to see him.

"We really appreciate all the things coach Chaney has done for us," said Jackson, who plays for the Minnesota Timberwolves. "He's always been very supportive. You know people watch him on television and see him hollering and screaming. They think coach Chaney is a madman. But they don't know he really cares about his players. He wants you to work as hard as you can."

Chaney understands hard work. He's been a blue-collar person most of his life. In 1951 Chaney was the Public League Player of the Year at Ben Franklin High School in Philadelphia. He was an NAIA All-American at Bethune-Cookman College in Daytona Beach, Florida. In 1953 he was the NAIA Tournament Most Valuable Player.

Jack "Cy" McClairen, assistant athletic director at Bethune-Cookman, was a teammate of Chaney's in college. McClairen remembers grabbing rebounds and throwing outlet passes to him.

"John Chaney was one of the greatest basketball players to ever play down here," McClairen said. "He brought a new basketball game to the South that we had never seen before. He sailed through the air. He had four or five different shots."

Added McClairen: "He's a great basketball coach. But I believe John was a better player. Unfortunately, he came at a time when it was difficult for blacks to play in the NBA."

After a season with the Harlem Globetrotters (1955), Chaney played in the Eastern Pro League with Sunbury (1955–63) and Williamsport (1963–66)—where he doubled as coach. He was a seven-time All-Star and MVP of the league All-Star Game in 1959 and 1960. He was twice named the league MVP.

"Man, he could play basketball," McClairen said. "You couldn't take the ball from him. He knew how to control the game. That's one of the reasons why he can coach. We're proud to have John in our [Bethune-Cookman] Hall of Fame."

Chaney started his coaching career with Williamsport of the Eastern Pro League in 1963. During that same time, he coached Philly's Sayre Junior High School basketball team. In 1966 he became Simon Gratz High School's basketball coach.

Leonard Poole played for Chaney at Simon Gratz. Poole, an All–Public League star, played his college basketball at East Stroudsburg State College, and is currently the head basketball coach at his alma mater. He frequently attends Temple practices.

"I enjoy listening to coach Chaney conduct his practices," Poole said. "He explains everything so thoroughly. He doesn't assume anything. He shows you exactly where to go on the court. And you better listen to him. If not, he's going to let you know it. I've listened to him for a long time. He's had a big impact on me."

In 1972 Chaney was hired as Cheyney State's head coach. He had a marvelous career coaching the Wolves. In fact, Cheyney's basketball program was one of the best in the nation among Division II schools. In addition to Chaney coaching the men's team, Vivian Stringer, who is now Rutgers' head coach, was in charge of the Lady Wolves.

"We played some great basketball at Cheyney," said Keith Johnson, who played for Chaney and is now an assistant coach at Coppin State under Ron "Fang" Mitchell, another Chaney disciple. "We had a lot of great teams there. And that was a tribute to him. I remember those days very well. Coach Stringer had a tremendous program. We both practiced in the same gym. He gave us a chance to be a part of a good tradition."

Chaney posted a win-loss mark of 225–59 (.792), guiding his team to eight NCAA Division II Tournament berths and a national championship in 1978. He had an amazing 10-year run with the Wolves.

"You know, coach Chaney has been coaching for a long time," said Milt Colston, who was a star guard on Cheyney's national championship team. "He's a member of the Basketball Hall of Fame. He's won a lot of games. But I'm pleased to say I played on his NCAA championship team. Winning a national title doesn't happen every day. He did a lot for Cheyney University. I was sorry to see him leave Cheyney. But a job like coaching Temple doesn't come around too often."

Chaney is one of three head coaches who have gone from a historically black college to a Division I school. Former Old Dominion head coach Jeff Capel toiled at Fayetteville State and North Carolina A&T prior to breaking into the big time. In 2002 Steve Merfeld left Hampton University for Evansville.

Dr. Peter Liacouras, former Temple president, noticed the success John Thompson had at Georgetown. In the spring of 1982, Liacouras got in touch with Sonny Hill, a good friend of Chaney and the Philadelphia 76ers' executive advisor, about a possible candidate. Hill quickly recommended Chaney.

Chaney took over the Owls' basketball program that summer. He doesn't see a lot of black college coaches getting the opportunity to work at the Division I level.

"I can't say that I've opened a lot of doors for black college coaches," Chaney said. "I was fortunate that Peter Liacouras gave me a call. But I don't see a lot of schools willing to take the chance on black college coaches.

"There's only been a couple to have a chance to work at a big school. I just don't see it happening. I've been here for 21 years. In that time, there have been very few opportunities."

Chaney hasn't changed much over the years. He still remembers the long bus rides to battle some of the best small college teams in the country. He can envision the classic Cheyney-Lincoln games, when more than four thousand fans crammed into the gyms to watch one of the oldest black college rivalries.

Every spring Chaney goes to the NCAA Final Four. He usually visits with the black college coaches and provides some words of encouragement.

"I like talking to the coaches," Chaney said. "If the black college coaches are organizing an event, I try to go. I've made plenty of friends throughout the years, like [Clarence] 'Big House' Gaines and Don Corbett. These guys were coaching when I was at Cheyney. Big House coached Winston-Salem for a long time. Corbett had a good career at North Carolina A&T. They were both outstanding coaches. I just hope black college coaches can continue to grow in the future. They deserve a chance to coach on any level."

Since arriving at Temple prior to the 1982–83 season, Chaney has guided the Owls to a win-loss record of 468–210 over 21 seasons.

"I was a little apprehensive my first year," Chaney said. "We had a lot of injuries that season. I was also coaching players I didn't bring with me. I really liked the kids we had at the time. We had Terence Stansbury, Jimmy McLaughlin, and Charlie Rayne. Granger Hall had major knee surgery. We had a losing season [14–15]. I was a little concerned."

Believe it or not, Chaney's first Temple team almost won the Atlantic 10 Conference Tournament crown, losing to West Virginia in the finals. Even though the Owls lost, that set the tone for the future.

In 1984 Temple made its first trip to the NCAA Tournament under Chaney. The Owls posted a 26–5 record and captured the A-10 Conference Tournament. In the first round, Temple upset St. John's, 65–63, on Stansbury's dramatic 22-foot shot at the buzzer. The Owls lost to the top-ranked University of North Carolina in the second round. The Tar Heels featured future NBA superstar Michael Jordan.

However, it was Temple's first victory in the NCAA Tournament since 1958. The Owls were the first Atlantic 10 team ever to go undefeated in regular-season play. Temple finished the season ranked 20th in the final Associated Press poll. Stansbury, who tallied 1,811 points in his Temple career, would become a first-round pick of the Dallas Mavericks.

Hall returned from a serious knee injury to be a force around the basket. Chaney was named the A-10 and USBWA (United States Basketball Writers Association) District I Coach of the Year.

"Terence Stansbury and Jimmy McLaughlin could really shoot the basketball," Chaney said. "They were some of the best shooters we've had here. Charlie Rayne was a great defender. He was a good rebounder. Granger was just a tireless worker. He spent a lot of time rehabilitating his knee. He came back from the injury and was a big reason why we went to the tournament."

Chaney's teams have made 20 postseason appearances in 21 years, including NCAA Tournament berths in 17 seasons and NIT bids in 1989, 2002, and 2003.

In the NCAA Tournament, his Temple teams have posted a win-loss record of 23–16 and made five appearances in regional finals games. In the Atlantic 10, Chaney guided the Owls to an all-time win-loss mark of 308–95, including seven regular-season titles and six conference tournament championships.

In 2001–02 the Owls compiled a 19–15 record while advancing to the semifinals of the NIT. Overall, his 31-year college coaching record is 693–269.

Chaney, a five-time Atlantic 10 Conference Coach of the Year (1984, 1985, 1987, 1988, 2000), was named the consensus (Associated Press, United Press International, USBWA, CNN/*USA Today*) National Coach of the Year.

Chaney has accomplished these feats with very little talent. Although Temple has produced several NBA players under Chaney, he rarely gets the top players. In his coaching career, he has signed only five McDonald's All-Americans: Mark Macon, Donald Hodge, Rick Brunson, Mark Karcher, and Kevin Lyde.

"Coach Chaney knows how to develop players," said Macon, who is the school's all-time leading scorer with 2,609 points. "In practice, he goes over things so well. I spent a lot of time just listening to him. I scored a lot of points in college. But coach Chaney made me a better defensive player. He raised the level of my game. I've seen him do it with others, too."

Macon, like many other players, was able to adapt to Chaney's coaching style and philosophy. Temple is not one of the most exciting teams. The Owls rarely run the fast break.

Chaney's teams walk the ball up court. They play mostly halfcourt basketball. The Owls take good care of the ball. Every year Chaney's teams are among the best at limiting their turnovers.

Defensively, Temple plays a matchup zone that drives opponents crazy. The zone forces teams to beat them with outside shooting. The defense closes off all passing lanes and causes teams to make difficult passes.

If you're a high school basketball star who is looking for a college where you can run up and down the court and take jump shots, then Temple is not the place.

John Chaney basketball is no-frills. It's nuts and bolts. Blue-collar and lunch pail. Tough. It's not Hollywood.

The team practices regularly at 5:30 A.M. This way the players don't have to worry about missing classes and study hall. Chaney doesn't allow his players to do any celebrating on the court. He doesn't permit his players to say anything to the officials.

Playing for Chaney means getting plenty of discipline. He's an old-school coach. And that's not because he's 71 years old. He has good standards and values. He has rules and regulations for his players. Moreover, he expects you to follow them.

"Coach doesn't put up with a lot of foolishness," said Aaron McKie, ex–Temple star who now plays for the Philadelphia 76ers. "If he asks you to do something, he expects you to do it. After playing for him, you know how to conduct yourself on and off the court."

Larry Brown, Detroit Pistons head coach, has known Chaney for many years. Brown coached against Chaney during his days at Kansas.

"His teams play the right way," Brown said. "They play great defense. They don't beat themselves. Temple has a rich basketball history. They've had some great players over the years. I'm very fortunate to have had a guy like Aaron who hustles and plays hard all the time. He's a great example of the types of players who have come from coach Chaney's program."

Chaney is all about helping the kids. He knows that every time he gives a scholarship to a player, there's another person who has a chance to improve himself. He's coached a lot of kids who have come from one-parent households. Some were raised by grandparents, uncles, and aunts, and others have come from the tough inner-city streets.

Although Chaney has sent close to 20 players to the NBA, professional basketball isn't an option for everybody. He realizes the importance of a good education. For that, many of his players come back to see him throughout the years.

"That's what makes me feel good," Chaney said. "To see them do well and to go back to help their families and communities. That means a lot to me."

The majority of Chaney's players go to summer school. Then, after classes, they participate in the Hank Gathers College League. Two years ago, Lynn Greer, the Owls' second all-time leading scorer, played for the USA basketball team, which captured a bronze medal at the 2001 World University Games in Beijing, China, although Chaney rarely lets his players compete on college all-star teams abroad. Prior to Greer, Aaron McKie, Eddie Jones, and Lynard Stewart were the only Temple players to have this opportunity.

"This was something I really wanted to do," Greer said. "It's just that I wanted to ask coach Chaney first. I was pleased when he said it was all right. This was a great experience for me. It's not every day you get a chance to go to China to play basketball."

Every now and then, Chaney has made a few exceptions. But one aspect of his coaching philosophy that hasn't changed is the rugged schedule his team plays every year. Nobody will ever accuse him of ducking the major college basketball powers. Chaney doesn't mind going on the road to play teams such as Duke, Kansas, UCLA, Michigan State, Indiana, and others.

"We've always played a tough schedule," Chaney said. "We've done it ever since I've been here. The schedule helps us get ready for the regular as well as the conference tournament. The competition is good. But more than anything, it helps our youngsters grow up."

The rough schedule provides Temple with a great deal of media exposure. The Owls have made numerous national television appearances. This gives them the visibility to recruit players around the country.

Chaney also knows that playing a competitive schedule is looked upon very favorably by the NCAA Tournament committee. When it comes to selecting the 64 teams to participate in the tournament, the committee looks at the strength of schedule, overall wins, and how well your team is playing heading into the conference tournament. Chaney's teams usually meet the criteria.

Winning games and making regular trips to the NCAA Tournament is what Chaney has done for 17 of his 21 years at Temple. That's a goal of his each season. He approaches every year with great enthusiasm.

The early-morning practices, the long road trips, and the pressure of winning games have a tendency to wear him down. But Chaney knows how to get away from the game. In the off-season, he usually plays tennis at Awbury Recreation Center near his Mt. Airy home.

"Coach loves to play tennis in the summer," Colston said. "It's a nice outlet for him. It takes him away from the stress and tension of basketball.

"He plays tennis for a couple of hours. After that, he brings out some food and everybody sits around and eats. Coach usually has some crabs."

Chaney has a famous line when it comes to relaxing during the summer months.

"I like to go sit under a tree and roast peanuts and drink beer and lie around, have fun with your friends, have fun with people that have fun with you," Chaney said. "That's like therapy for me."

It doesn't take much to make Chaney happy. He didn't get into coaching to earn a lot of money.

He started coaching in the Eastern League. Then he became a teacher and spent time coaching and teaching in the Philadelphia Public School System. After that, former Cheyney president Dr. Wade Wilson called him to teach and coach at one of the nation's oldest black colleges. In a decade at Cheyney, he won a national championship, National Division II Coach of the Year honors, and the State of Pennsylvania Distinguished Faculty Award in 1979.

"I was very fortunate that Peter Liacouras gave me an opportunity," Chaney said. "I was very happy at Cheyney State. I wasn't looking to go anywhere, but this was a good opportunity for me. If it wasn't for him, I don't know if I would ever have been able to coach at a school like Temple."

The Owls' Hall of Fame coach has done quite well at Temple. His fortunes could be even larger. Unlike most coaches, Chaney doesn't have a big sneaker contract. He's not interested in having his own television and radio show. He doesn't charge for speaking engagements.

Moreover, Chaney and his wife, Jeanne, reside in a small home in Philadelphia. Chaney's hobbies include going to the city's Italian Market and buying clothes. He has an extensive tie collection—more than 500 from some of the best designers in the world.

"I don't spend a lot of money on things," Chaney said, "but I love ties. I've bought ties from places like Barney's in New York that cost a lot of money. I used to give my ties away after a loss. It's just that I started losing too many games over the last few years. It was costing me plenty of money. So, I had to stop that."

Chaney's other vice is eating. According to the Owls basketball guide, he names his top five cities that offer the best food.

"Of course, Philly will always be number one for the cheese steaks and hoagies," Chaney stated. "I like Maryland for crabs and the great seafood. I like those big strong crabs that do push-ups. Louisiana is great for its Cajun rice. New England—Boston and Maine, I guess—is great for its lobster. And I love the barbecue in Memphis and Kansas City. They're both great, but I think I'd give the edge to Memphis."

Chaney has a tremendous appreciation for food and clothing. He grew up in Jacksonville, Florida, where he lived in the housing projects. He spent most of his youth down south until his mother, stepbrother, stepsister, and he moved to Philadelphia to live with his stepfather, who was working in a shipyard in Chester, Pennsylvania. His family lived at 17th and Ellsworth Streets in South Philly.

"I'll never forget those days," Chaney said. "We lived in a small house right near the corner. We didn't have a lot of money. When I went to Ben Franklin High School, I only had enough money to ride one way. Sometimes I would ride up and walk back. I never had enough money to do both."

Life certainly hasn't been all peaches and cream for Chaney. In addition to receiving a dose of poverty as a kid, he's experienced some tragic losses as an adult.

Jim Maloney, Chaney's good friend and longtime Temple assistant basketball coach, died on May 3, 1996, after suffering a heart attack while driving a car in Philadelphia. He was 62 years old. Maloney was the father of former Penn and NBA shooting guard Matt Maloney.

"I always hoped the Lord would call me before my brother," Chaney said during the eulogy for Maloney's funeral services. "The Lord needed Jim to prepare a place for all of us."

When Chaney was coaching at Cheyney State, he and Maloney—who was then an assistant for former Temple coach Don Casey—would go on recruiting trips together. They were very good friends, and the bond between them got even stronger once Chaney arrived at Temple.

For the entire 1996–97 season, Chaney kept the seat next to him, where Maloney used to sit, empty. The season was dedicated to him.

Maloney's death should have been enough, but more tragedy followed. The following year Chaney's top recruit, Marvin Webster Jr., passed away. Webster, son of former NBA shotblocker Marvin Webster, died of a heart attack in mid-August.

After that, Chaney's former Independent League basketball coach, Victor Harris, passed away. Then, Ennis Cosby, son of actor-comedian and good friend Bill Cosby, was shot to death along a Los Angeles freeway. Ennis had attended the John Chaney–Sonny Hill Basketball Camp as a youngster.

In spite of so many tragedies, Chaney still perseveres. He's always been a fighter. There's nothing phony about him. He believes in standing up for what he believes in. And he believes in standing for what is right.

His battles with the NCAA have been well documented over the years. He told the NCAA that Proposition 48 and 42 were unfair to a number of blacks, disadvantaged youngsters, and poor kids from the inner city. As a former public school teacher, Chaney knows it's difficult to impose rigid standards on students who have struggled to learn in the early grades.

"There should be more emphasis on helping kids in the primary grades," Chaney said. "You have to spend more time with the kids from K through 12. The NCAA makes a lot of money. If they could give some of the money to the schools and communities where most of the players come from, that would make a big difference."

When the building of the Apollo, which was later renamed the Liacouras Center after former president Peter Liacouras, became a political football, Chaney let his feelings be known.

He had built the Owls basketball program into a national power. The team was playing in McGonigle Hall, a thirty-nine hundred–seat arena. The Liacouras Center seats more than ten thousand fans. The new arena, which opened during the 1997–98 season, has attracted some outstanding teams—such as Michigan State, Maryland, Wisconsin, Indiana, and Memphis—to the Temple campus on North Broad Street. The Liacouras Center has raised the profile of Temple basketball.

"Our program outgrew McGonigle Hall," Nate Blackwell said. "Coach had a lot to do with that. We needed a bigger arena."

As the Owls grew under Chaney, his accomplishments continued to be recognized around the country. And then, on May
30, 2001, he received a call from the Naismith Basketball Hall
of Fame.

Chaney had been selected with former NBA star Moses
Malone and Duke head coach Mike Krzyzewski to enter the
Hall of Fame. He was officially inducted during a ceremony
at the Springfield Civic Center in Springfield, Massachusetts,
on October 5, 2001.

Chaney's presenter was former Georgetown coach John
Thompson, a Hall of Famer who is now a color analyst for
NBA games on TNT. Chaney and Thompson have known
each other for years. Temple has faced Georgetown in the
NCAA Tournament as well as some nonconference games.

"I can't say enough about John," Thompson said during
the ceremony, "but the things that I respect him for are things
that you don't always see in the coaching fraternity. One thing
that I respect him for is the fact that he's a great coach. That
goes without saying, and I guess that's the reason why a lot of
folks think he's here.

"The other reason why I have a great deal of respect for
him is the fact that he's a tremendous teacher. And I think a
lot of times when guys do the things that they have to do to
prepare a person for the world that they have to live in today,
it's so often misunderstood. But John has done a tremendous
job directing young men in the right direction.

"The third thing, which is probably one of the most significant things to me, is that while he was doing a very difficult
job, he didn't neglect his obligation to address social issues that
pertained to so many kids who were not under his care. And
that's an enormous distraction."

The ceremony ran the gamut of emotions, from laughter to tears. Chaney started out by talking about humility.

"I can remember coming out of my house and getting into my car," he said. "I have a very small house. I'm in a row home. I've been there all my life, although my wife would like us to get out. My neighbors would not like to see me leave.

"But a bus had been rerouted, because they had some kind of construction work going on, and the bus was rerouted and came down my street filled with people. And I run out of my house to get in my car, and the bus stops, and the bus driver gets off the bus and says to me, 'Aren't you John Chaney?' I said, 'Yes.' And he said, 'I thought you'd be living in a mansion.'

"The people on the bus said, 'Damn John Chaney. We're going to be late for work. Get your ass back in the bus!' Now if that doesn't tell you what kind of a person you are, then nothing will."

Chaney mentioned his high school coach, who was a major reason why he went to college.

"I had a great high school coach, a Jewish man by the name of Sam Browne, who passed a way a couple years ago, who would not allow me to do anything but go to college," he said. "And he worked extremely hard trying to convince my parents that I should go to college. I remember one day in the summer, he would find time to buy us clothes, because we were very poor, take us out to the Poconos, to the mountains, where we'd be free from gangs and all the problems of the city.

"And he convinced them that I had an opportunity to go to school. That opportunity came one day before [Clarence] 'Big House' Gaines (former Winston-Salem State and Hall of Fame coach) came looking for me. He came one day late, and I found myself at Bethune-Cookman College, one of the first land grant colleges in America, where a black woman founded that school."

Chaney went on to recognize people such as Sonny Hill; Speedy Morris (former La Salle head coach, who now coaches Philly's St. Joseph's Prep); his current coaches; former assistant coach Nate Blackwell; Dan Leibovitz; his business manager John DiSangro; his secretary Essie Davis; and Dr. Anthony Pinnie, a high school friend.

He gave a special mention to Tom Gola and to coaches Al McGuire, Jim Maloney, Vivian Stringer, Dean Demopoulos, and Bill Ellerbee for supporting him throughout the years. He also thanked his wife, Jeanne; daughter, Pamela; sons John and Darryl; and four grandchildren.

Chaney ended the ceremony with a picture titled "Dreams," which hangs in his office. The picture shows a young black boy, asleep in bed with one arm around a football. Chaney read the inscription. "It says here, 'I being poor have only my dreams; I spread my dreams under your feet; tread softly, because you just might tread on my dreams.'"

For most coaches, the Hall of Fame induction ceremony usually signals the end of their career. But the train that drives Chaney keeps right on moving. The 2002–03 season was his 31st in the coaching profession.

Chaney has no immediate plans to retire. Coaching is what he enjoys.

"I haven't thought about leaving," Chaney said. "I'll be around as long as my health is all right. And as long as we can continue to bring in youngsters who are willing to listen and learn, then I'll be around for a while."

CHAPTER 1

Coach's Pride and Joy

When they met John Chaney during the 1989–90 season, Aaron McKie and Eddie Jones didn't expect to become rich and famous. McKie, a 6'5" guard and clutch performer, helped the Philadelphia 76ers to the NBA Finals in 2001. He also received the league's Sixth Man Award that same year. These accomplishments were especially sweet for McKie, who, as a North Philadelphia youngster, was a big fan of the Sixers.

His solid defense, clutch shots, winning attitude, and professionalism have been well received in his hometown. McKie, 30, was selected by the Portland Trail Blazers with the 17th pick of the 1994 NBA Draft. In his third NBA season, he was traded with Randolph Childress and Reggie Jordan to the Detroit Pistons for Stacey Augmon. In December 1997 the Pistons dealt McKie, Theo Ratliff, and a first-round draft choice to the Sixers for Jerry Stackhouse and Eric Montross.

McKie played three seasons at Temple after sitting out his freshman year for failing to meet the NCAA Prop 42 requirements. He finished his college career tied with Mike Vreeswyk for sixth on the school's all-time scoring list with 1,650 points. Only NBA great Guy Rodgers scored more points over three Temple seasons.

Jones, a 6'6" guard, played 4½ seasons with the Los Angeles Lakers. In his first season, he was named MVP of the NBA Rookie Game after scoring 25 points. Jones, 31, also participated in the 1997 and 1998 NBA All-Star Games. During the 1998–99 season, he was traded with Elden Campbell to the Charlotte Hornets for Glen Rice, J. R. Reid, and B. J. Armstrong. After one year with the Hornets, who have since moved to New Orleans, Jones was traded with Anthony Mason, Ricky Davis, and Dale Ellis to the Miami Heat for P. J. Brown, Jamal Mashburn, Otis Thorpe, Tim James, and Rodney Buford.

Jones played three years at Temple, where he became the school's 13th-leading scorer (1,470 points) despite sitting out his freshman year. In 1994 the Lakers made him the number ten pick in the first round of the NBA Draft. He was Jerry West's only lottery pick as GM of the Lakers.

Jones and McKie started their collegiate careers in 1991 as victims of Proposition 42. They had to sit out a season and pay their way. Today Jones and McKie sponsor teams in the Sonny Hill Community Involvement League. Jones has started his own foundation. McKie has bought new homes for his aunt, Rose Key, and mother, Pearl McKie. McKie resides in Haverford, Pennsylvania. Jones also has purchased a home for his mother, Frances Jones. Jones resides in Weston, Florida, approximately 45 miles from Miami.

Both players have earned respect around the NBA. "I've known Aaron and Eddie since my days at Duke," said Grant Hill, star forward for the Orlando Magic. "I remember playing against them in college. They're both good players. You can tell they've learned a lot from John Chaney. Aaron used to play for us [with the Pistons]. I remember one time I got hurt and Aaron replaced me in the starting lineup. He got a triple-double that game. You can always count on him to give you a great effort."

Theo Ratliff, who teamed with Aaron in Philadelphia and now plays for the Atlanta Hawks, feels McKie is not only a good player, but also a terrific person off the court. McKie made a huge impression on him when Ratliff was first sent to Philadelphia by agent Joel Bell.

"Aaron is a very caring person," Ratliff said. "I know all the things he went through when he was younger. I know he didn't have it easy coming up. Before I got drafted in the NBA, I met him through the little practice sessions in the summertime. I came out to work with John Hardnett, and that's how I met Aaron. John holds workouts for college and pro players around the city. Aaron is a down-to-earth person. He's very aware of this [NBA career] being a short-term situation. He's taken care of his family. I really don't know coach Chaney. But everything Aaron tells me about him, he would do anything for him."

McKie's caring and understanding personality has touched Sixers teammate Allen Iverson, who won the NBA Most Valuable Player Award in 2001. Iverson is the most exciting player in the NBA. He also has been in and out of trouble throughout his career.

Several years ago, Iverson and former Sixers head coach Larry Brown had a very difficult time getting along with each other. In fact, it got to a point where it looked like Brown was going to trade Iverson. During those struggles, Iverson needed someone levelheaded. McKie was there for him.

"Aaron is a good friend of mine," Iverson said. "He's a guy I can always talk to. He's made a big impact on me. He's a great person for the city, the Sixers organization, and the kids. I really admire the way he carries himself."

Iverson is not alone. McKie has impressed a lot of people in the Sixers organization. It's well documented that Brown is a big fan of McKie.

"He's very coachable," Brown said. "He plays the right way. You hear Sonny Hill and coach Chaney talk about him all the time. He's not only a good player, but a great person."

Eric Snow, one of McKie's teammates, won the 2000 NBA Sportsmanship Award for his conduct on the court. Snow received $25,000 and a trophy from the NBA. He gave half the money to his middle school in Canton, Ohio. The other portion went to McKie's alma mater, Simon Gratz.

"I wanted to do something good for Aaron," Snow said. "He's done so much for people in the area. If the students at his school can aspire to be like him, they'll turn out to be great individuals."

Jones played one season for coach Paul Silas (now head coach of the Cleveland Cavaliers) when he was in Charlotte. Silas acquired him in a trade with the Lakers. Before Jones put on a Hornets uniform, Silas spoke to Chaney.

"I gave John a call when Eddie came here," Silas said. "John told me I wouldn't have any problems with Eddie. And he was right. Eddie was a great player for us.

"I remember John talking about him and Aaron McKie. He gives these guys plenty of guidance. That's why they know how to conduct themselves."

Del Harris, former Lakers head coach and now an assistant coach with the Dallas Mavericks, enjoyed coaching Jones. Harris could see the Chaney influence right away.

"You only had to explain things to Eddie once," Harris said. "He came ready to play all the time. He's a great team player. I think a lot of these attributes come from John Chaney. He's established a good foundation for players like Eddie and others. When you get a player from Temple, you know he's going to be sound fundamentally and well disciplined." McKie and Jones owe a lot to Chaney.

 ## Eddie's Thoughts

I don't know where I would be without coach Chaney. He didn't know I was going to play in the NBA, but coach Chaney knew that going to college would help me become a well-rounded person. It would give me a chance to do something good with my life. Whenever I got down, I could always call him. Sometimes it would be late at night. It didn't matter. Coach Chaney would always try to help me. He's spent a whole career helping people. He's taken a particular interest in helping the less fortunate. I'm glad he took an interest in me.

 ## Aaron's Thoughts

He's made a big difference in my life. He realized things weren't all peaches and cream for me. But coach Chaney never let me feel like I couldn't make it. Coach Chaney knows how hard it is for somebody to succeed without a good education. He knows society can squeeze you out of a lot of opportunities if you don't have a college education. Although I'm doing well playing in the NBA, once my career is over I'll be ready for the next step.

CHAPTER 2

First Impressions of John Chaney

M ost of Chaney's players have been poor and have come from one- or no-parent families—kids who have struggled to survive with limited resources. Chaney has recruited carefree, middle-class, two-parent honor students, too, but few of them have chosen Temple. Those few have thrived and helped their less fortunate teammates.

Chaney can identify with underprivileged youngsters because he had to overcome some of the same obstacles. He was raised by his mother and stepfather in Jacksonville, Florida, and South Philadelphia. Chaney took odd jobs to help his family put food on the table.

Chaney was a sensational basketball player for Philadelphia's Ben Franklin High School. In 1951 he was named Public League Player of the Year. But Chaney didn't receive one scholarship offer from any Philadelphia college. He wound up playing for Bethune-Cookman College, a small black school in Daytona Beach, Florida. He was an NAIA All-American.

Chaney was fortunate to go to college. He didn't have terrific grades in high school. He wasn't placed in a college preparatory program. A Ben Franklin guidance counselor said he wasn't college material. Chaney has encouraged kids to go to college. He realizes that if someone hadn't given him a chance, he wouldn't have succeeded in life. Under current NCAA rules, Division I Bethune-Cookman wouldn't have given Chaney a chance.

He's a man who wants to get the most out of his players. It's similar to the person who is trying to get the best pitcher of orange juice. He squeezes the orange until all the juice runs out. That's the way Chaney coaches the game. If you watch him on the sidelines, he's living and dying with every call the official makes. With sweat pouring off him, tie pulled down, and sleeves rolled up, Chaney grimaces whenever a player throws the ball away. In case you didn't know, turnovers are not permitted at Temple.

Whatever you do, protect the basketball. Don't throw it away. And you better play defense. He doesn't care about behind-the-back passes, between-the-legs dribbling, or dunks. That doesn't excite him. He wants players to do the things that help them win.

These things all center around the basic fundamentals. Chaney's style of play isn't attractive to a lot of high school players today. It seems like most kids are more interested in running up and down the court. They want to take off from the foul line and make a spectacular dunk. Or they want to shoot a three-pointer with three players hanging all over them.

They want to do anything that will get them a 10-second highlight spot on the local TV news—or better yet, ESPN's *SportsCenter*. These guys are not Temple players. Basically, this means they're not John Chaney–type players.

Not everybody can play for him. He likes discipline. He wants kids who are going to listen. He doesn't want kids who think they're the greatest thing since Wilt Chamberlain.

It takes a special kind of person to play for Chaney. You have to practice at 5:30 A.M. He places heavy emphasis on education. If he finds out that you're not going to class or study hall, he'll throw you off the team.

Some college coaches are only interested in winning basketball games, making money, and appearing on television shows to promote themselves. That's not Chaney. He wants kids who are respectful of others and know how to conduct themselves off the court.

Some people see his demeanor and think of Bobby Knight, former Indiana head coach who now coaches Texas Tech. Knight has won national championships. He has coached such great players as Isiah Thomas, Quinn Buckner, and Scott May. He's also known for throwing chairs and berating players.

"Some people think I'm the black Bobby Knight," Chaney said.

That's scary to a lot of high school players and coaches. Chaney is not like Knight. Both coaches are tough, but Chaney has a different personality. With that being said, Chaney is noted for his outbursts. He does read his team the riot act on a regular basis.

"I don't want him yelling at me," said one Philadelphia basketball standout. "Plus, he doesn't let you run and play your game."

Chaney has recruited some kids—such as Johnny Miller, Johnnie Conic, and Ronald Blackshear—who ended up transferring to another school.

Jonathan Haynes was one of Chaney's best recruits and a good friend of McKie. In 1991 Chaney signed Haynes, who was regarded by many high school sportswriters as one of the best guards in the country, on a full scholarship. He played his scholastic basketball at Philadelphia's Germantown Friends School.

Haynes, a 6'3" player, could score any time he wanted to on the court. He could dribble the ball around any defender. His hands were among the quickest in the city. With his long arms, he could pick anybody's pocket. In addition, he scored more than 2,000 points in his high school career.

In spite of Haynes' brilliant skills, he wasn't a good fit for Temple. He excelled in the open court, where he could make spectacular plays. That's not the way Temple plays basketball.

Haynes, an intelligent player, had trouble with the Owls' defensive-minded, slow-down, bump-and-grind style of play. When it appeared he wasn't going to receive a lot of playing time, he decided to transfer. He would eventually finish his career at Villanova, where he would play against Temple during his senior year.

Chaney wants his players to dream. He doesn't want to take their dreams away. In North Philadelphia, where McKie was reared, dreams vanish quickly. Aaron hails from 10th Street and Susquehanna Avenue, one of the worst sections in the city. In his neighborhood, you can see drug deals being made in the open, kids hanging out all night, sometimes in vacant homes.

Aaron is the youngest of five children of Woodrow and Pearl McKie. He got involved in sports at a young age. He used to watch his father play softball. He became very attached to his father. Unfortunately, McKie's father died of a heart attack and a stroke when Aaron was nine. During that time, McKie was living in the Germantown section of the city.

McKie was in ninth grade when his elderly aunt, Rose Key, took him into her home at 10th and Susquehanna. Aunt Rose was a highly religious widow with no children of her own.

John Hardnett and Bill Ellerbee also played significant roles in Aaron's development as a young man. Hardnett was McKie's coach in the Sonny Hill League and an all-year mentor. Ellerbee was his coach at Simon Gratz High School (and is currently an assistant on Chaney's staff).

"As a youngster, Aaron went through quite a bit in his life," Ellerbee said. "It was hard for him to lose his father at a young age. I've known Aaron since he was about eight years old. He played on my 12-and-under team at Belfield Recreation Center. Before Aaron officially joined the team, he used to sneak in my car with the rest of the players to come to the games. I used to tell him he couldn't come because he wasn't on the team. He asked if he could be the manager. I said that would be fine since all the kids like him.

"He really liked basketball. You could tell he was going to be a good player. The game brought a lot of joy in his life. Basketball was a good outlet for him, but I was really worried about him. His family situation wasn't very solid. I can remember times when he didn't want to go home. I dropped him off one night after a basketball game. The next thing I knew, he was walking down the street. So, I knew something had to be done.

"Aaron was in the ninth grade at Lincoln High School. He wasn't doing particularly well in school. He was a young man with all kinds of potential. He moved in with his Aunt Rose in North Philly. She really did a nice job of providing a home for him.

"Once Aaron came here, he worked very hard on and off the field. He was not only a great basketball player, but Aaron could play some baseball, too. He was one of the best pitchers in the Public League. He was scouted by the Houston Astros and the Chicago White Sox. I remember when John Chaney was recruiting him to come to Temple. Aaron told him he was on the baseball team here. John thought Aaron was a catcher. So, he said to him, 'You're not wearing the tools of ignorance are you?' Aaron said, 'No, Coach, I'm a pitcher.' Basically, Aaron is a guy who battled on and off the field. And he never once thought about throwing in the towel."

Ellerbee would spend a lot of time with McKie during the day. In the evening, McKie would be in Hardnett's basement lifting weights and watching television. Pooh Richardson and Doug Overton also developed leg strength with Hardnett's weights.

"Aaron is one of my all-time favorite people," Hardnett said. "He's always appreciated everything. I've known Aaron since he was eight years old. He played on my Sonny Hill League team. He came to all my workouts. I followed Aaron in high school and college. I realized Aaron didn't have very much in terms of resources. I tried to help him as much as I could. If there was anybody in the world to have a reason to complain, it was Aaron. He's gone through a lot.

"Nevertheless, he's never complained about his situation. Aaron was fortunate to have some people who really cared about him. For example, his Aunt Rose really liked him. She was a strict disciplinarian, too. She didn't trust too many people. Aaron didn't have a radio, so I bought him one. Aunt Rose wouldn't let him bring it in the house until she saw a receipt. I turned my car upside down trying to find the receipt. She didn't want any stolen merchandise in her house. They do a lot of stealing in her neighborhood. I found the receipt and everything was all right.

"Family is very important to him. He has taken care of his mother, Aunt Rose, his nephews—Shaun and Khari McKie. I've been fortunate to work with both of them.

"Aaron used to eat dinner at my house, and I'd drive him home. My mother [Lucille Hardnett] used to say, 'Aaron is going to be a success, because he has such good character.' We had no idea he'd wind up in the NBA. We hoped he'd have a chance to go to college."

Although McKie was a hard worker and a talented player, he wasn't highly recruited. Three teammates on Hardnett's Medics team—Jonathan Haynes, Carlin Warley, and Harry Moore—went to the prestigious Nike All-America Camp in Princeton. This camp attracted the country's finest high school players. Hardnett took McKie to watch.

"I told Aaron, 'Don't worry about not going to the camps,'" Hardnett said. "I could see the disappointment on his face. I think what really hurt was that all his friends were there. But Aaron just continued to work hard and play well."

Aaron sharpened his skills in the Sonny Hill League in preparation for a big senior year.

McKie led Simon Gratz to its first Public League championship since 1939. He averaged 18.9 points, 9.9 rebounds, and 7.2 assists a game as the Bulldogs finished with a terrific 26–4 record. He was named the Herb Good Club's Public League Player of the Year. Public League coaches, however, chose Jules Mastbaum Tech's Kevin Benton (Delaware, Liberty University) as the senior to be honored in the Markward Club.

It wasn't until the Albert C. Donofrio Classic in Conshohocken that Temple recruited him. McKie received co-MVP honors after the Sonny Hill Seniors won the championship.

Jones, like McKie, didn't grow up in the lap of luxury. His parents, Charles and Francis, were divorced when he was attending Blanche Ely High School in Pompano Beach, Florida. Eddie maintained a great relationship with his father. Charles came to most of his games in high school. After his father died of cancer,

Eddie thought about quitting school to help take care of his mother. But his mother told him to stay in school and dedicate his final season to his father. That's exactly what he did.

"Everybody was really concerned about Eddie," said Wade Edmond, Ely High School head basketball coach. "He was very close to his father. Eddie's father was really proud of him; he always talked about him. Eddie had a rough time dealing with his passing. He did get over it. But Eddie had a lot of help from his mother and all the people in the community. They really liked him."

Jones, a slender, 6'6", quick-footed, high-flying forward, wasn't the franchise at Ely. The big name at his high school was Kevin McDougal. Eddie wasn't recruited heavily until the Florida Shootout in Kissimmee, Florida. Eddie averaged 25 points, 10 rebounds, and five blocked shots per game. Temple was able to wrestle him away from other major college powers because of Chaney.

"When Eddie played in the 10th grade, he was just a regular kid," Edmond said. "In his junior year, he was a role player. Our big star was Kevin McDougal, who ended up playing football at Notre Dame. But I decided to make Eddie the focal point of the offense his senior year. He was terrific. He scored inside as well as outside. He ran the floor. He did all the spectacular things you see him do on television. Eddie wasn't that good right away. He did a lot on his own by simply playing in the gym. He would play for hours and hours, working on all parts of his game.

"Dean Demopoulos [Temple assistant basketball coach] saw him play in the Florida Shootout. Temple wanted him very badly. John Chaney came down for a visit. Eddie's mother liked Chaney quite a bit. But I have to give our principal, Mr. James L. Jones, some credit. Mr. Jones went to Bethune-Cookman with Chaney. He knew John was a great person. He knew Eddie would be in good hands with him. So, Temple came highly recommended from him."

During the 1989–90 season, McKie and Jones were being recruited by Temple. They had heard a lot of things about Chaney from different people. Some good. Some bad. But McKie and Jones quickly found out that Chaney was not the ogre his enemies had made him out to be. McKie knew a lot more about Chaney than Jones did. After all, McKie lived about six blocks from Temple. McKie was fundamentally sound. More of a workmanlike player. Nothing fancy, but very sound in every facet of the game. Jones was a very explosive player. He's one of the most athletic players ever recruited by Chaney. But McKie and Jones found out exactly what kind of person they were going to play for before they signed with Temple. A man with a sense of humor who cares deeply for his players and is a no-nonsense person.

 ## Aaron's Thoughts

First of all, I was in awe of him. I had heard so much about him. My high school coach at Simon Gratz, Bill Ellerbee, told me about him. I know he used to coach at Gratz. Coach Ellerbee told me he was a disciplinarian. In other words, he didn't play. So, I knew he was tough.

But coach Chaney really cares about his players. I used to watch Temple play at the Palestra. At the time, I was maybe 11 or 12 years old. I was playing peewee basketball. Our team used to get tickets to watch some of the Big 5 games. This was before I started playing in the Sonny Hill League. I liked the way Temple played the game. They were never out of control. They dictated the pace of the game.

Coach Chaney would call a play and everybody would go to where they were supposed to be on the court. I liked the way he handled the team. I said to myself I would love to play for him. John Hardnett and Herm Rogul used to get tickets for me to watch them play at McGonigle Hall. I was in high school at the time. There were some exciting games at McGonigle Hall. I kept saying to myself that I played in McGonigle Hall over the summer in the Sonny Hill League and it would be great to play here all year long.

I just wanted to play for coach Chaney. I wanted to come to Temple badly. I was only being recruited by Coppin State. They had a great program in Baltimore. They're coached by Ron "Fang" Mitchell, who is a disciple of coach Chaney. I was headed for Coppin State until Temple started recruiting me. They came to see me play in the Conshohocken Tournament. Apparently, coach Chaney was interested in me. I started to get real excited about coming to Temple. Then, when they offered me a scholarship, I was really happy. This was my chance to play for one of the best coaches in the country.

But one thing I'll always remember during the recruiting process was meeting Bill Cosby at Veterans Stadium during a Temple football game. Coach Chaney introduced me to Bill Cosby. I couldn't believe it. Here was a guy who grew up in North Philadelphia, just like me, and now he's successful. Of course, that might be putting it mildly. But I was really impressed with him. I don't know how many people know that Cosby grew up in the Richard Allen Housing Projects. He gives a lot of people hope, just like coach Chaney.

I knew Coach was tough. I knew I had to get up at 5:30 in the morning to go to practice. But I knew it would be worth it. Coach Chaney used to tell us his father would make him wash his car at 5:30 A.M. It didn't bother me getting up early for practice. I mean, it was hard at first, but I got used to it after a while. Actually, I knew that was something I had to do before I got there. Everybody was talking about coach Chaney's early practices. So, I knew I had to wipe the sleep out of my eyes and walk down Broad Street to McGonigle Hall.

We used to have donuts and orange juice at practice. You know Coach had to have some breakfast for us. He loves food. I've seen him pick tomatoes and look at them like, "Is this a good one?" I'm not too familiar with his cooking. But like I said, he likes to eat. People don't realize he's a funny guy. He has a great sense of humor.

Coach is a guy who lets you know where he stands immediately. He sits down and talks to you about life. He explains what's expected of you as a player and as a person. He tells you the importance of going to class. If you have a problem, don't hesitate to come to see him. He's a no-nonsense guy. But the man cares about you. That meant a lot to me coming from North Philly. Basically, he gave me a chance. That was all I needed. I wanted to do well for my family and friends. But I wanted him to be proud of me, too.

I think Jonathan [Haynes] could have played for coach Chaney. He just wanted to play right away. I felt really bad when he decided to transfer to Villanova. Jon is one of my best friends. He did a lot for me. I was very close with his family. We played in the Sonny Hill League. But things just didn't work out for him.

Family is very important to me. That's why I really appreciate what my Aunt Rose did for me. She provided me with a place to live when I needed it the most. Once again, family is everything. That's why I try to help everyone out, from my nephews, Khari and Shaun, right to my mother and Aunt Rose.

❝ Eddie's Thoughts

I met coach Chaney when he came down to Florida. He seemed like he was a Southern guy. Then, I found out Coach was from Jacksonville and played his college basketball for Bethune-Cookman in Daytona Beach. At the time, I was being recruited by Florida State, Georgia Tech, Michigan, and a lot of Division I schools across the country. I didn't think about playing for Temple until I met coach Chaney. He explained everything very thoroughly about the Temple program. He talked about discipline, respect, responsibility, and things like that.

But coach Chaney left a great impression on my mother. He made her laugh during his recruiting visit. I could see where my mother was real comfortable with him. He talked about life, education, and basketball. After he left the house, I knew I was going to Temple. My high school coach, Wade Edmond, was a John Chaney clone. He was tough on everybody. So, I was ready for Coach's hollering and screaming.

I remember one time we were playing La Salle, we were ahead by 20 points. That game, I was guarding Kareem Townes. The game was pretty much in hand. All of sudden, Kareem was dribbling up court. I was guarding him loosely. The next thing I knew, he was launching a shot from 30 feet. The ball went right in the basket. Coach Chaney jumped off the bench and started hollering at me. He shouted, "Play some defense! Play some defense, Eddie!" I said, "Coach, he hit a 40-footer." Coach said, "I don't care, play some defense."

That was the only time I can remember Coach hollering at me. Now, he gave Aaron a tough time. Coach stayed on him. But my situation was different. It wasn't that I was special or anything like that. If Coach hollers at you or speaks to you, it's because he wants you to do better. He wants you to do more. He doesn't want you to accept being average. He wants you to strive for as much as possible.

Plus, he does things for a reason. Some people think he hollers and screams for nothing. That's not true at all. He has a method to his madness. He wants you to be better. It's hard for some people to understand that. But that's where Coach is misunderstood.

I came to Temple during the Spring Fling. Mark Macon was my host. He and coach Chaney were very close. And they're still very close today. Everybody knew Mark Macon. He was one of the best players in the country. He showed me around the campus. I didn't meet Bill Cosby or anybody famous. Macon told me how coach Chaney really cares about the players.

I could tell from talking to Mark Macon that Chaney was a father figure to him. That had an impact on me, too. My father died when I was in high school. I really miss him. So, I was happy to be playing for somebody like Coach. Somebody who is going to be tough, but also understanding.

My stepfather [E. J. Thigpen] has been very good to my mother [Frances]. As you know, Coach likes to eat. My stepfather used to make cakes. Coach would always ask me for one of his cakes. He made all kinds of cakes. Pound cakes, lemon cakes, you name it. So he used to make some for Coach and send them up. Coach would eat them and tell me how good they were. But then he would start asking for cakes all the time. I told Coach, "You're going to have to start paying for these cakes. They take a lot of time. You got to get in the kitchen, turn the oven on, and bake them." My step-father didn't mind doing it. He's a good person, just like coach Chaney.

CHAPTER 3

They Couldn't Go Many Places, So They Chose Temple

Mckie and Jones were good enough high school basket-ball players to be recruited by a number of Division I schools. Unfortunately, because they were unable to meet the NCAA requirements of Proposition 48, which mandated that a student-athlete must score a 700 on the Scholastic Aptitude Test or 18 on the American College Test, their options were very limited. Jones had attracted interest from Tennessee, Georgia Tech, Alabama, and Michigan. McKie was recruited by Coppin State, Duquesne, and Ohio University. Temple was their best bet.

John Chaney had already coached Ernest Pollard, Duane Causwell, Donald Hodge, Mark Strickland, and Michael Harden, who were victims of Proposition 48. Chaney was totally against the NCAA ruling. He felt as though the requirements were unfair to poor, inner-city youngsters, denying them an opportunity to get an education. Jones and McKie didn't like being labeled "Prop 48." They used the label as an incentive to do well in the classroom and on the court. Proposition 48 at least allowed its victims to get scholarships.

In the beginning, most people thought Chaney was being unnecessarily outspoken about Proposition 48 and Proposition 42. In 1990 the NCAA decided to revise Proposition 42. Two years later, the Presidents Commission put together a package that appeared to really have a negative impact, called Proposition 16. This policy governs the NCAA initial eligibility requirements for student-athletes at more than 300 Division I colleges.

Implemented in 1995, it is more restrictive than Proposition 48, according to the National Center for Fair and Open Testing. High school graduates who do not meet Prop 16's requirements are precluded from participating in intercollegiate competition and may be denied athletic scholarships.

To qualify for full eligibility, student-athletes must have a 2.0 grade point average in 13 "core" courses and an SAT of 1010 or a combined ACT of 86. Students with lower test scores need higher course GPAs. The minimum test score for students with a GPA of 2.5 or higher is 820 SAT/68 ACT.

For some students, meeting the academic requirements of a B-/C+ average in high school and an 820 on the SAT may seem relatively easy. But for many youngsters from disadvantaged backgrounds, it's a struggle to meet these requirements. That's one of the reasons why Chaney battled the NCAA and anybody else over Propositions 48 and 42. He believed the NCAA was overstepping its bounds.

Chaney felt the NCAA should stick to regulating intercollegiate athletics rather than telling colleges which students to accept. Chaney believed Propositions 48 and 42 discriminated against youngsters at the bottom rung of the ladder.

Chaney was a major spokesman on these topics, appearing on such national television programs as *Good Morning America* and *Nightline*. He also wrote articles for *The New York Times* and *Sports Illustrated* concerning this matter.

"Propositions 48 and 42 have punished a lot of kids," Chaney said at the time. "They don't need punishment. They need encouragement.

"These rules hurt a lot of black kids who don't have the money to pay their way to school. Let's not deny a kid an opportunity to learn because of his economic background. It's easy to educate kids who are academically talented and come from good families. But let's give everybody a chance to go to college."

According to the National Center for Fair and Open Testing, an organization based in Cambridge, Massachusetts, the data on student-athletes' academic performance prior to the 1986 implementation of Proposition 48 reveal the discriminatory impact of these rules. The data, reanalyzed by the McIntosh Commission on Fair Play in Student Athlete Admissions, show that had Proposition 48 been in effect in 1984 and 1985, it would have denied full eligibility to 47 percent of the African-American student-athletes who went on to graduate, but just 8 percent of the white student-athletes. More recent NCAA research shows that the test score requirement disqualifies African-American student-athletes at a rate that's nine to ten times greater than the rate for white students.

Russ Gough, a noted sports ethicist, had some strong comments regarding the SAT.

"There is a strong correlation between family income and standardized test scores," he wrote in a 1995 *Washington Post* story. "The NCAA's own studies have completely ignored this well-documented and well-known correlation. The upshot here is that, under the present rule structure, the NCAA might as well throw out its standardized test score requirements and simply allow a freshman to play or not play on the basis of his family's income."

McKie and Jones are typical of most student-athletes who were unable to meet the academic standards set by the NCAA. Both players were educated at "neighborhood" public high schools from the inner city. McKie is a graduate of Simon Gratz High School located in the rugged section of North Philadelphia. Jones is an alumnus of Blanche Ely School in Pompano Beach, Florida, which is located near Fort Lauderdale. It's one of the largest schools in predominantly black Broward County.

Neither school would be confused with being a magnet or special admissions school for academically talented students. These schools reach out to youngsters who don't possess all the amenities of kids from upper-middle-class families—that is, two-parent households, good jobs, single-family homes, and personal computers. McKie and Jones were not privy to such resources. But one thing's for sure: these are the kind of players Chaney recruits.

❝ Aaron's Thoughts

I don't kill myself thinking about Proposition 48. It happened for a reason. It did give me an opportunity to adjust to college life. I had a chance to get together with Eddie. But I have to tell you, my freshman year was really hard. It wasn't easy sitting out. I would go to the games and say to myself, "Man, I wish I was out there playing." I could see myself now sitting up in the stands of McGonigle Hall watching Mark Macon, Donald Hodge, Mark Strickland, and everybody play. I usually sat with Eddie. We would just turn to each other and shake our heads. Sometimes we'd leave and go back to the dorm to listen to Jay Norman's [former Temple radio analyst] comments on the game. Jay made us laugh.

Proposition 48 is really unfair to a lot of inner-city kids and kids who don't have a strong educational background. I went to Simon Gratz. I worked extremely hard in high school. I did pretty well in the classroom. I got a lot of help from coach Ellerbee and all the other teachers and guidance counselors. It's just that I couldn't pass the SAT. I don't understand why they put so much emphasis on that exam. It doesn't mean you can't do college work.

I got through Temple by going to class, studying, and working hard. It had nothing to do with SAT scores. It's cut-and-dried in college. If you don't go to class and study, you're not going to make it. College requires discipline on the part of students. You don't have parents standing over top of you saying, "You have a biology class to go to at 10:00 A.M." It's up to you to get there and do the work.

That's why Proposition 48 isn't a true measure of how a student will perform in college. I'm living proof of that. Coach Chaney has been trying to tell people for years about Proposition 48. I was ready to play for a coach who clearly understands the struggles of inner-city kids. I grew up in North Philadelphia. Things weren't easy for me. Coach Chaney knows what it's like to grow up poor and without a chance to make it in life. He had to work hard for everything. He didn't have anything handed to him. But Coach is willing give a person a chance to succeed. He's taken a lot of Prop 48s over the years. He's been criticized for it, too. But coach Chaney doesn't care. He's going to continue to give kids a chance to make it. He's not going to let anybody go by the wayside.

Eddie's Thoughts

I didn't like being called a Prop 48. I didn't care for the label at all. It makes you feel bad. It's like having pins and needles stuck in your foot. That's how bad it hurts. I tried to use Proposition 48 as motivation. I knew I was capable of doing the work. I never doubted my ability to do well in the classroom. It's just that I needed to buckle down. I didn't do as well in my books like I should have. In high school, I didn't have any problems with English, math, or history. I just needed to put forth a better effort in my books.

I definitely worked extremely hard at Temple. Aaron and I spent a lot of time studying together. We wanted to be eligible to play as sophomores. It was really frustrating sitting out as freshmen. Our first year, Temple went to the Final Eight and lost to North Carolina. We had some great players on that team, like Mark Macon, Mark Strickland, Donald Hodge, and Mik Kilgore. If Aaron and I weren't Prop 48s, we may have gone to the Final Four that year.

It was a long season my first year at Temple. As a Prop 48, the only thing you can do is study and work out. You can't practice with the team. But coach Chaney really made Aaron and myself feel a part of the team. We used to visit him in his office all the time. Sometimes we didn't even want anything. We just wanted to find out what was going on with the team. Coach Chaney, Dean Demopoulos, and Jim Maloney always had time for us. We just wanted to talk to somebody. It gets very lonely on the sidelines. But it was nice to have a guy like Aaron to help me through my first year.

I never liked the perception of being a Prop 48. It makes you feel like you're stupid. That's why Aaron and I were so determined to do well. We wanted to succeed based on what we went through our first year. I majored in sports management. This was a good major for me. I think it's helped me a lot as a professional athlete.

Aaron and I played in Temple's Intramural League in Pearson Hall, right next to McGonigle Hall. Before we started playing in the league, we would always work out together. After we completed our studies, we usually headed for the gym.

But playing intramurals was a lot of fun. Every time we played a game, the gym would be packed. The students would come to the games to see us play. They would say, "Hey, they're going to be playing for Temple next year." Aaron and I put on quite a show. There weren't a lot of good basketball players in the league. They had a few guys who could really play the game, but that was it. The league kept us in shape during the season. It wasn't like playing for coach Chaney. We could do whatever we wanted on the court. We didn't have to worry about turnovers. I can't remember too much more about playing intramurals. I know my team won the championship. I also know the league, Aaron, coach Chaney, and the staff helped me get through my freshman year. I really appreciate it, too.

CHAPTER 4

Sophomore Year

After sitting out their freshman year, Aaron McKie and Eddie Jones were anxious to play for John Chaney in 1991–92. Temple was coming off a Final Eight season. The Owls weren't expected to challenge for a national championship or to get to the Final Four. Temple's key returning players were Mik Kilgore, Mark Strickland, and Victor Carstarphen. The Owls had lost Mark Macon, Donald Hodge, Michael Harden, and Chris Lovelace. Macon was a lottery pick by the Denver Nuggets. Hodge and Lovelace left school early. Hodge was a second-round pick by the Dallas Mavericks, while Lovelace played pro basketball overseas.

Chaney had recruited Rick Brunson, a 6'4" All-America guard from Salem, Massachusetts. Brunson was recruited by Kentucky and other major college programs. Hodge was replaced by 6'10" Frazier Johnson, a junior-college transfer from Arkansas.

The Owls had the second toughest nonconference schedule in the country in 1991–92, with powerhouses such as Arizona, Kansas, Wake Forest, Tulane, Memphis State, Villanova, and Illinois on the bill. The Owls went 17–13, 11–5 in the A-10. Temple was invited to the NCAA Tournament for the eighth time in Chaney's 10 years as coach. The bid kept alive a streak of nine straight postseason appearances for the Owls. The big win for Temple that season was the 65–63 victory at Memphis State in the Tomb of Doom. The Owls set a school record with 19 three-pointers (the fifth highest total in NCAA history) against George Washington.

McKie and Jones were magnificent in their initial college season, combining to average more than 25 points, 10 rebounds, four assists, and four steals per game.

Temple's season concluded with a first-round 73–66 loss to Michigan in the NCAA Tournament. The Wolverines started the freshmen Fab Five of All-Americans Chris Webber, Juwan Howard, Jalen Rose, Ray Jackson, and Jimmy King. Michigan would lose to Duke in the NCAA title game. McKie and Jones received a good taste of college basketball as sophomores. Both players talked about wanting to make a big impact right away.

Playing the game was easy for them. The big adjustment for McKie and Jones was managing their time during the season. They had to make arrangements with their professors to get all their work completed before leaving town.

Occasionally, they would have to go home after a road trip to take an exam. During one stretch, Temple played West Virginia, Rutgers, St. Joseph's, and Duquesne away from home in the course of nine days. McKie and Jones didn't want to fall behind in their studies. This was in the back of their minds all the time. They knew the doubters were out there. McKie and Jones didn't want to fail.

The Owls stayed in a hotel in Center City during the Atlantic 10 Conference Tournament. This arrangement allowed the team to be away from the campus but remain focused on the game. The conference tournament is the beginning of March Madness.

Concentration was a big thing for McKie and Jones. Temple is one of the biggest draws in college basketball. The school can thank Chaney for that recognition. He has turned the Owls' basketball program into one of the most respected across the country.

On this night, Temple would face Big 5 rival St. Joseph's in the first round of the A-10 Tournament. More than seven thousand fans crammed into the Palestra. When the St. Joseph's basketball team came out of the locker room, the fans cheered, "Let's go St. Joe! Let's go St. Joe!"

A few minutes later, Temple's squad graced the court for its warm-up drills. The Owls faithful began to chant, "Let's go Temple! Let's go Temple!" It was pandemonium before the officials blew the whistle.

"This is the kind of stuff you dream about," said Temple star Mik Kilgore at the time. "This was a Big 5 game in a play-off atmosphere. I'm just glad everything turned out all right for us."

Temple defeated St. Joseph's 74–59 to get that all-important 17th win. The Owls advanced to the second round of the tournament, but only to lose to West Virginia, 44–41, in an uninspiring, low-scoring game.

After being eliminated from the conference tournament, McKie and Jones headed back to campus to catch up on some schoolwork. They spent the next three days wondering if they would go to the NCAA Tournament. Temple was considered a bubble team. That's a team that doesn't have a great season overall and has to hold its breath until the NCAA committee calls its name during the selection process.

"I hope we go somewhere," Kilgore said. "I don't want to miss the tournament my senior year."

Every year Temple holds a party for the basketball team, coaches, and alumni on campus with hopes of them receiving a bid. In 1992 the party was held in Sullivan Hall. There were a lot of alumni and supporters talking about the tournament. Several television sets were tuned into CBS Sports. Everybody had a plate of food in their hands. Then, right before the selection show came on, Chaney, Maloney, Demopoulos, and the rest of the team entered the room and sat on the couch. Everybody was still eating—except the players.

"I can't eat until I find out who we play," Brunson said, "but somebody save me a sandwich."

They could hardly wait for CBS to start the program. The players and coaches knew that if the team was not one of the 64 teams invited to the tournament, Temple would be headed to the less-prestigious National Invitation Tournament (NIT).

"Nobody wants to go to the NIT," said a Temple alumnus. "We want to make the big dance."

The local TV news went off. It was 6:30 P.M. and CBS Selection Sunday came on. Jim Nantz and Billy Packer, CBS sportscasters, began to go through the pairings and the seeding for the East. All of a sudden, the announcement came that Temple would play Michigan in the first round. A loud cheer from all the fans erupted in the room. McKie and Jones looked at each other in jubilation.

❝ Aaron's Thoughts

It was a long time coming for me. I know it was for Eddie, too. I remember playing in the Sonny Hill College League telling Jonathan Haynes, Carlin Warley, and all my friends that it wouldn't be long now. This was in August. The next thing I knew school had begun. The basketball team started informal workouts. Basically, we would just scrimmage against each other in McGonigle Hall or Pearson Hall, whichever gym was available. On Friday nights leading up to the season, Eddie, myself, and John Hardnett used to practice in the gym. John Hardnett stayed on top of us. He wanted Eddie and me to be ready when college basketball practice started in October. We used to shoot jump shots for hours. We used to shoot the ball so much that when we came to a certain spot on the floor, we knew the ball was going in the basket. We were well prepared for college basketball season.

The opening of college basketball season is a big celebration on some campuses. Some colleges have drawings, music, food, games, and other things leading up to midnight. After midnight the team comes out and practices. There's about eight thousand fans in the arena as the season officially begins.

But that doesn't happen at Temple. There's no "Midnight Madness" in North Philly. Coach Chaney doesn't go for all that fanfare. He wants you at practice the next morning. The first day of practice, he does a lot of talking. I mean, Coach is telling one story after the other. I wish I could remember some of them. But I do remember him saying, "Don't let yourself fall into a false sense of security." The other thing is you've got to have the patience of Job. I think coach Chaney learned that in church.

The practices were very competitive. I can't remember anybody not playing hard. As most people know, coach Chaney doesn't like turnovers in the games. Well, he doesn't like them in practices, either. I remember him hollering at me, Mik, or Victor if we turned the ball over. Coach Chaney worked us hard during the preseason. He drilled us over and over again. He believes you learn from repetition. I know Eddie and I had all the plays down pat. We got off to a good start. We won like our first four games. Then, we started to be inconsistent. That was driving coach Chaney right up the wall.

We would win two games, then we would lose two games. This went on throughout most of the season. Now, we did have a tough schedule. Coach Chaney wants to play the best. Plus, he doesn't run from anybody who's good and wants to play Temple. He'll play you at home or on the road. We were 16–11 heading into the A-10 Tournament. Our biggest win was against Memphis State. They had Penny Hardaway, one of the best players in college basketball. He was a first-round pick of the Orlando Magic. [Hardaway was actually drafted in the first round by Golden State. He was traded to the Orlando Magic on draft night and currently plays for the Phoenix Suns.] So far, he's had a great pro career. But we beat Penny's team on the road. It was a huge win for us.

But I can still remember people saying we needed another to get into the NCAA Tournament. In the first round of the A-10 Tournament, we had to play St. Joseph's, a conference rival and a Big 5 team. Also, they had beaten us once that season. I kept saying to myself, "I want to go to the NCAA Tournament." I told Eddie, Mik, Vic, and Mark Strickland how badly I wanted to go to the tournament. I didn't want to hear anything about the NIT. Mik, Vic, and Mark were seniors. They wanted to go, too. They also wanted to win for coach Chaney. He's developed a reputation as a "tournament coach."

Eddie's Thoughts

I came off the bench my sophomore year. It didn't
bother me. I had sat out the year before. I was ready
to contribute. I tried to give the team a lift. I told coach
Chaney whenever he needed me, I was ready to play.

You know, people don't realize college is different
from high school. You don't have people standing over
top of you making sure you go to class. That's why
coach Chaney leaves you with no excuses. We practice
at 5:30 A.M. After practice you've got time to study and
go to class. But you have to accept the responsibility.
You have to be disciplined, too. You can't go to class
one day, then turn around and not go the next. As you
can see, coach Chaney taught me about being responsible and disciplined in my first year of playing ball.
People don't know we had to study on the road. We
didn't just play basketball. I had to stay on top of everything. I waited too long to play for Temple. I didn't want
to let myself down. I didn't want to let coach Chaney
down. He gave me a chance to come here.

It's funny, a lot of people didn't think this was one
of coach Chaney's better teams. But I thought we had a
pretty good team. Our shooting wasn't always there.

We did hit some outside shots. One thing we could
always do is play defense. The matchup zone used to
kill everybody. That's why nobody wants to play
Temple. Coach Chaney does a great job of teaching the
fundamentals of the defense. We don't give up anything
in the paint. If you're going to beat us, you've got to do
it from three-point range. I used to love to see teams
throw the ball in the corners. Once the ball went into

the corners, I knew there were only one or two places they could throw the ball. That's how I got my steals.

It's tough playing against our zone. It's even harder if you don't see the zone on a regular basis. I liked to see the expressions on players' faces, trying to crack the defense. I'm sure they probably think there's eight guys on the court instead of five.

Coach Chaney used to stay on us about playing good defense. I can hear him now. "Aaron, what are you doing over there? You belong on the wing. Mik, don't let him shoot. Go get him." It was like that the whole year. You get used to coach Chaney hollering. You start listening a little more. You try to understand some of the things he's telling you.

You can see he really cares. You want to win for him. This was my first year. I wasn't one of the older guys. But I wanted to take coach Chaney all the way. I remember playing Michigan in the first round. It was one of the biggest matchups in the tournament. Everybody had their eyes on the "Fab Five." Actually, that's all you heard about during the season. I remember Rick Brunson giving us some tips on the Fab Five. Rick played against some of those guys in the McDonald's All-America Game. We played them extremely well in the tournament. It was a real close game. We just made turnovers down the stretch. We took some bad shots and that killed us. If we could have beaten them, we would've gone a long way. They have three guys in the NBA from that team—Chris Webber, Juwan Howard, and Jalen Rose. But Temple had four guys from that team—myself, Aaron, Mark, and Rick—go on to the NBA. That's why it wasn't a bad team.

CHAPTER 5

Aaron's Year

Temple wasn't expected to have a great 1992–93 season. The Owls were definitely capable of making the NCAA Tournament, but nobody thought they would explode on the national college basketball scene.

This team finished with a 20–13 overall record, won the Big 5 City Series championship, and advanced to the NCAA Final Eight. In the tournament, Temple defeated Missouri (75–61), Santa Clara (68–57), and Vanderbilt (67–59). Once again, Temple faced Michigan in the tournament and fell to the "Fab Five" (77–72) in the West Region championship game.

This was the year Aaron McKie and Eddie Jones really emerged as outstanding college basketball players. McKie and Jones were each named to the All–West Region team. Jones averaged 21.3 points and McKie 20.5 in the tournament. Aaron tallied 680 points, making him only the seventh Temple player to score more than 600 points. McKie was named Atlantic 10 Conference Player of the Year and the Big 5's Most Outstanding Player. He received honorable mention All-America honors from the Associated Press. Jones also made All–Big 5.

Rick Brunson, the Owls' highly touted star from Salem, Massachusetts, played a big role in the team's success. The 6'3" guard was able to put aside his frustrations and stay with the Temple program.

Immediately following the 1991–92 season, Brunson had requested his release from the school. He wanted to play closer to home. He decided to transfer to Boston College, only to change his mind and return to Temple. Chaney's decision to allow Brunson back into the fold would prove to be crucial. During the 1992–93 season, Victor Carstarphen, Temple's starting point guard, broke the fibula bone in his left leg. The injury occurred against Cincinnati during the sixth game of the season.

At that point, Brunson emerged as the team's playmaker. He became the perfect complement to McKie and Jones. Brunson, a southpaw lead guard, would dribble the ball down the center of the court. He usually stopped on a dime and dished the ball off to either McKie or Jones. They couldn't have achieved their success without Brunson's steady ball handling and savvy play.

Although McKie and Jones came into their own as players, they remember some of the year's twists and turns that made the season special.

66 Aaron's Thoughts

We had a lot of things happen that year. I had a pretty good year. I got Player of the Year in the conference. That was a big award to me. The Atlantic 10 was no slouch. We had some good players in the A-10 during my career, like Carlin Warley [St. Joseph's], Lou Roe [Massachusetts], Harry Moore [St. Bonaventure], Bernard Blunt [St. Joseph's], and, of course, Eddie. We knew each other extremely well. We were all friendly rivals, but very competitive. Every summer we played against each other in the Sonny Hill College League. During the summer months, you could go down to [Temple's] McGonigle Hall and see a player from our conference on the court. Like I said, this was a great honor.

But I was pleased with the way the team responded to some difficult things. For example, we lost Victor Carstarphen, our starting point, with a broken leg. He broke his leg against Cincinnati.

It was ironic because Victor used to play for them. He transferred to Temple from Cincinnati. Victor missed a lot of games [20]. He didn't come back until the NCAA Tournament. The other thing that happened was we lost our center, Frazier Johnson [who left school due to academic reasons following the seventh game]. I know losing Frazier really hurt coach Chaney. He really liked him. Frazier was a junior-college transfer. He played for us my sophomore year. He was just starting to come around offensively and defensively. Unfortunately, he had to leave. I'm sure a lot of people said you can't give people like him a chance. But coach Chaney believes in giving everybody a chance. I came to Temple because he gave me a chance.

But sometimes good things come as a result of something bad. When Victor went down, Rick Brunson stepped up as our starting point guard. Rick came to Temple with a big reputation [McDonald's All-American]. Coach Chaney didn't hesitate to put him in the starting lineup. He responded very well. He took a lot of pressure off Eddie and myself. We had three legitimate scorers on the floor. It's not easy playing point guard for coach Chaney. He doesn't want you to turn the ball over. That drives him crazy. Nevertheless, Rick was able to give us ball handling and scoring.

When Frazier left, coach Chaney had to give Derrick Battie and William Cunningham some playing time. They were just freshmen at the time, but Coach knew we really needed them. Cunningham and Battie had good size. Battie was a little more talented than Cunningham. He could do a few more things around the basket. William was a little stronger. If he got the ball close to the basket, he could usually score.

Once again, I have to give coach Chaney a lot of credit for keeping the team together. We could have packed it in for the season. But we didn't hang our heads. We took what we had and kept right on playing. And remember, we're playing some of the best teams in the country.

Like the year before, we were inconsistent for a good part of the season. We were around the .500 mark (10–10) at midseason. I remember people saying we had to win our conference tournament to get into the NCAA playoffs. I didn't pay them any mind. You see, people don't realize that Temple's a tournament team. They should look at coach Chaney's record. We hardly lose during the month of February.

We felt pretty confident playing against the conference teams. We needed some big nonconference wins. We got two big ones, Memphis State and Tulane. That gave us a lot of momentum going into the conference tournament. We played well in the A-10 Conference Tournament. The only thing was Massachusetts beat us in the championship game. UMass was tough. They were developing a pretty good basketball program. The loss didn't hurt us in the big picture. We were able to get to the NCAA Tournament. That's coach Chaney's goal every year. He wants to get to the tournament. If he can do that, he knows there's a chance we could win some games.

And that's exactly what happened. We went to the Final Eight. If we didn't have to play Michigan, we would have gone to the Final Four. My junior year was a showcase for me. After the season, I was chosen to play for Team USA, a group of college players who were going into their final year of eligibility. I wasn't sure coach Chaney was going to let me play for the team, but I was really excited about being picked. So, coach Chaney checked with my academic advisers. They told him it was all right for me to go.

My coach was P. J. Carlesimo, who, believe it or not, was famous before the Latrell Sprewell incident. P.J. was the head coach of Seton Hall. He also coached me in the NBA with the Portland Trail Blazers. P.J. is a tough coach. He definitely gets on you about things. But I played for coach Chaney, so P.J. really didn't bother me.

I had a good experience playing for Team USA. I played with some great players, like Michael Finley, Eric Montross, and Jason Kidd. Billy McCaffrey and I were roommates. Billy is from Allentown, Pennsylvania. He used to come and play in the Sonny Hill League. We went on a tour of Europe and played against national teams from Italy, Belgium, Spain, Germany, and Holland.

I never thought I would have an opportunity to play basketball in Europe. This doesn't happen every day to kids from North Philly. I'm glad coach Chaney let me go. I had a great time. But I would have traded everything for a national championship. That's how much I think of coach Chaney.

 ## Eddie's Thoughts

I hated to lose to Michigan twice. We had just lost to them my sophomore year. It was frustrating to me. It was hard for coach Chaney, too. I remember he got a technical foul in the last few minutes. I think if we had had one more big man, we would have been all right. We got as much as we could from William Cunningham, Derrick Battie, and Jason Ivey. You can't take anything away from Michigan. They had a great team. It's just that we got so close to going to the Final Four. It's definitely frustrating. It takes you a couple of days to get over all the excitement from the tournament.

It was exciting for us from the time our name was mentioned on Selection Sunday right up to the time we lost to Michigan. We had a good run in the tournament, beating Missouri, Santa Clara, and Vanderbilt. I don't think anybody had us going too far. We won the first two games in Salt Lake City. Then, we had to go to Seattle and play the next two games. That was a lot of traveling for us. I have to admit, once the tournament ended I was pretty tired. But I would have had some energy to get to the Final Four.

Every year, something inspires you to play harder for coach Chaney. I'll never forget the look on his face after we lost to Wake Forest [106–69]. He was really upset. That was probably one of his worst defeats in his coaching career. I'll never forget that game. They came into McGonigle Hall and crushed us. The game was on national television. Everybody around the country saw Temple get spanked. Usually teams were very uncomfortable playing in McGonigle Hall. It was loud, the fans were right on top of the court. We played there all the time. We played there in the summer. It didn't matter to Rodney Rogers and Randolph Childress from Wake Forest. They just did a number on us. They weren't intimidated at all. Then again, I didn't think we played very well that day.

I don't remember coach Chaney saying much after the game. But you could tell he wasn't happy. I guess he felt the scoreboard told the story. After the Wake Forest game, we may have lost two more games the rest of the season going into the conference tournament. We definitely turned it up a couple notches. We wanted to play well. And that's basically what we did.

It's funny how a lot of people forgot about the Wake Forest game because of how well we played in the tournament. I've heard coach Chaney say people remember what they see last. I think most Temple fans remember how far we went in the NCAA playoffs. They remember that more than the loss to Michigan in the Final Eight.

One thing I'll always remember is playing in the [7 Up Shootout] tournament in Orlando. We played Louisville and Florida State in the tournament. We beat Louisville [68–53] and lost to Florida State [91–80] in the championship. We should have won the tournament. We led throughout most of the game against Florida State. But they came up really big in overtime.

Nonetheless it was a nice homecoming for me. I had a lot of family and friends who came to the game. I played most of my college games in the Northeast. We did play some games in the South, but only one in Florida. I have to thank coach Chaney for that. He always tries to play a game near the hometown of one of his players. Believe it or not, it was a home game for him, too. I'm sure he probably had some family and friends from Jacksonville, Florida. He may have even had some friends and former classmates from Bethune-Cookman there. He has a lot of friends in Florida.

CHAPTER 6

Eddie's Year

Aaron McKie and Eddie Jones believed their senior year was the season Temple would go to the NCAA Final Four. Rick Brunson, Derrick Battie, William Cunningham, and Jason Ivey all returned from the previous year's Final Eight squad. The 1993–94 Owls finished second in the Atlantic 10 Conference with a 12–4 record. They were Big 5 champions with an overall 23–8 mark.

McKie and Jones were named honorable mention All-Americans. McKie was a John Wooden Award finalist and a first-team All–Atlantic 10 Conference selection. He tallied 1,650 points in his career, second to Guy Rodgers among three-year Owls and sixth on Temple's all-time scoring list.

Jones was named Atlantic 10 Player of the Year. He finished 13th at Temple with 1,470 points and became the first Owl to record 100 career assists and 100 blocked shots. In spite of the brilliant seasons from McKie and Jones and even Brunson, who made second-team All–Atlantic 10, their season ended too soon.

The Owls' 23 wins—John Chaney's ninth 20-win season—concluded with a 61–39 romp over Drexel and 67–58 loss to Indiana in the NCAA Tournament. The loss ended the collegiate careers of McKie and Jones, but that final season with Chaney included big victories over national powers Kansas and Louisville.

However, the event that received the most notoriety was Temple's 56–55 loss at the University of Massachusetts on February 13, 1994. Chaney met the media first and mainly complimented the winning team. He was with his players when he heard that John Calipari, then the Massachusetts head coach, had complained about the officiating. Chaney exploded and rumbled into the postgame news conference, threatening Calipari.

The television cameras were rolling during the entire tirade. Shortly thereafter, people around the country were watching Chaney lose his temper.

Then Temple president Peter Liacouras suspended Chaney for one game. Since then, Chaney has apologized for his actions.

"I made a terrible mistake," Chaney said. "I was wrong. I should have handled the situation better."

This wasn't the first time Chaney has gone after an opposing coach. In 1982 he grabbed Dr. Tom Davis, then the Stanford coach.

After the Stanford incident, Chaney said, "When Cheyney was being treated poorly on the road, I sometimes acted crazy to the refs to start giving us some calls and to get the fans to yell at me and leave my players alone. Keith Johnson would grab me and carry me back. When I tried my act at Stanford, Granger [Hall] and Terence [Stansbury] and the others looked at me like I was crazy and stepped away. I hadn't prepared them for this part of the game."

He also had a run-in with Gary Gimelstob, former head coach of George Washington. To Chaney's credit, he hasn't been involved in skirmishes since the Calipari incident.

However, seemingly every local and national television station had shown highlights of Chaney's outburst. Temple and Massachusetts, like all conference teams, play each other twice. This was the Owls' first meeting with the Minutemen. The fans couldn't wait for the second game.

They weren't the only ones. The second game, played at McGonigle Hall, was on ESPN. Fans were all over the building. Even filmmaker Spike Lee was in the house. Lee is a big fan of Chaney. He had arranged a couple of cameo appearances for Chaney in his movie *He Got Game*.

People thought Chaney was going to explode again, but that didn't happen. He had already apologized to Calipari on the phone.

Both coaches came out and shook hands before the start of the game to break the tension. Calipari was quite dapper. He looked like he had stepped out of a Brooks Brothers catalog. Chaney wore a classic argyle sweater with one of his expensive designer ties.

After the 1994 season, Calipari left Massachusetts for the NBA's New Jersey Nets. He lasted only two and a half seasons before New Jersey fired him. Larry Brown, former Philadelphia 76ers head coach, hired him as an assistant coach. He spent five months with the Sixers, then was lured back into the college game by the University of Memphis.

Subsequently, Chaney scheduled a game with Memphis during Calipari's first season, a game won by the Owls. In 2002 Temple lost to Memphis twice, once during the regular season and again in the NIT semifinals.

Temple and Massachusetts had developed quite a rivalry in the Atlantic 10 Conference. The games were very intense. In fact, the Owls lost to the Minutemen in the first 1993–94 game on a Mike Williams banked jump shot in the final seconds.

McKie and Jones remember the Calipari incident quite well. They remember the look on Chaney's face during the last regular-season game against Massachusetts on February 24 at Temple's McGonigle Hall. And they remember Chaney's reaction when McKie and Jones walked off the court for the last time in the NCAA Tournament.

 ## Eddie's Thoughts

We should have gone a lot farther. Aaron, Rick, and myself were just one game away from the Final Four the year before. I wanted to be on the first team to take coach Chaney to the Final Four. I tease coach Chaney sometimes about our loss. I tell him he was outcoached by Bobby Knight. Indiana had a pretty good team. They had Damon Bailey as well as Alan Henderson, who now plays for the Atlanta Hawks. I didn't think Indiana had one of its best teams, but they had a good game against our matchup. They hit a lot of three-pointers [10-of-20]. That really opened things up for them inside. We had to go out and chase the three-point shooters. That's when we knew we were in trouble.

It's sad losing your last game. You know, it's your final game with coach Chaney. He's a very emotional person. People look at him and say he's a madman. But I'll never forget coming off the court at the end of the Indiana game and getting a big hug from him. That hug has stayed with me. It's kind of hard to describe the feeling. The hug from coach Chaney says a lot of

things. I think it says, "I really appreciate all the
things you've done." It also says you're ready for the
next step. For coach Chaney's players, that means finishing your education, getting a job, or possibly going
on to the pros.

No matter how you look at it, it's emotional. That's
how it is with Coach. Actually my last year was a very
emotional season for him.

I think that was evident with both games against
Massachusetts. Emotion runs both ways with him. It
doesn't take much to set him off. I didn't think Coach
minded losing to UMass. I mean, they had a good team.
But I think Calipari should have left it at that. I don't
think he should have talked about the officiating. That's
what got everything started. The next thing I knew,
coach Chaney ran into his postgame press conference
hollering at Calipari. I don't think coach Chaney has
ever forgotten that situation. I don't think he holds a
grudge against him. Coach knows how to move on from
things like that.

The second time we played them was Senior Night. It
was at McGonigle Hall. The place was packed. We must
have had about four thousand fans watching the game.
The media was really building the game up because of
the incident. Everybody thought something was going to
happen between coach Chaney and John Calipari. But
they both came out and shook hands. I guess that took
the edge off.

That's when coach Chaney headed out to the halfcourt. At that point, I knew the ceremony was going to
start for Aaron and myself. My mother and stepfather
had come up for the game. Coach hugged me and my

mother and stepfather. I could see the tears in his eyes. Like I said, it's sad. Then again, there's a lot of joy, too. It was nice that my mother and stepfather could be there. Coach Chaney has developed a family atmosphere. As a matter of fact, I consider Temple a part of my family. Where I go, Temple goes. Where Temple goes, I go.

After we had our pictures taken and the starters were announced, the game was under way. Once again, it was another close game. I think we lost by one point [51–50]. But there was no confrontation. And that was good. We didn't need any negative publicity.

I learned a lot from these situations. The one thing is, you can't lose it. Coach Chaney knows he made a mistake. Everybody still loves him. But you've got to stay under control.

 ## Aaron's Thoughts

I didn't want the season to end. I wanted to keep playing for coach Chaney. Of course, when they took me off the court against Indiana with a few minutes left in the game, I knew my playing days for Temple were over.

As I walked toward the bench, coach Chaney reached out and hugged me. At that time, I know a lot of things went through my mind. I thought about how hard I had worked in the classroom. I thought about all the things I had to go through my freshman year. I thought about how fortunate I was to play in the NCAA Tournament for three straight years. And then I thought none of this would have been possible if not for coach Chaney. He gave me an opportunity to play for him. He believed in me.

He really cares about people. He's not into making a lot of money. He does very well now. I'm sure Temple takes care of him. But coach Chaney could make a lot of money if he wanted to. He could have his own radio and television shows. He could do all kinds of personal appearances. But that's not him.

That's why I felt bad about the Calipari situation. I know a lot of people saw coach Chaney go after him. He lost it for a few minutes. I think the reason why coach Chaney went off was because he thought Calipari was grandstanding. Calipari thought his team got some bad calls. I don't think coach Chaney liked him complaining about the officiating. I'm sorry the situation occurred. I know Coach apologized for the outburst. He made a mistake. But, like I said, it's the perception. Some people think he's a wild man. That's not true.

Now, Coach will get on you about not going to class or study hall or even about not playing defense. You have to be tough to play for him. I know coach Chaney got on me pretty good. I could hear him now: "We're going to put you on the wing. Do you think you can guard somebody there?" I would just nod my head. Then I would say, "Coach, I can play anybody over here." I miss that kind of dialogue.

My last year went very quickly. I can't explain it. I don't know if it was the anticipation of playing in the tournament. I can't put my finger on it. Before I knew it, Senior Night was here. That's always a special game.

It's a touching moment for Coach. He knows the seniors are getting ready to leave him. I had my Aunt Rose and my three sisters—Jackie, Sandy, and Traci—with me.

I know coach Chaney was really happy for Eddie and myself. He was happy to see us succeed, but sorry to see us leave.

CHAPTER 7

First-Round Draft Picks

John Chaney couldn't have been any prouder of Aaron McKie and Eddie Jones on Wednesday, June 29, 1994. That night, Jones was selected by the Lakers with the 10th pick, McKie by the Trail Blazers with the 17th pick.

"I'm really happy for them," Chaney said. "I was hoping everything would work out for them. I spoke to a lot of NBA teams, and they all said how much they liked Aaron and Eddie. Both of them have done everything they're supposed to do. This is a special moment for them."

This was the first time in Temple and Big 5 history that two players from the same school were taken in the first round.

During Chaney's 21 years at Temple, he has produced a number of players who have gone on to the NBA, including Terence Stansbury, Nate Blackwell, Tim Perry, Mark Macon, Donald Hodge, Ramon Rivas, Duane Causwell, Rick Brunson, Mark Strickland, Pepe Sanchez, Marc Jackson, and William Cunningham, along with McKie and Jones. He doesn't concern himself with sending guys to the pros. Chaney is interested in giving young men an opportunity to play basketball and get a good education. McKie and Jones certainly understand his philosophy.

"Good things happened to good people," Hardnett said. "Aaron and Eddie are good people. They worked hard and good things happened for them."

With McKie and Jones being drafted by different teams, this marked the first time they wouldn't be together. McKie and Jones were one of the best combinations in college basketball. They knew each other's moves extremely well. They were like peanut butter and jelly. Now, after four years, they would be going their separate ways.

McKie and Jones were excited about being first-round picks. But as with most of their accolades, they seemed to take everything in stride.

There wasn't much question as to where they were going to be drafted. Most NBA scouts had them pegged as first-rounders. Other college basketball players had to compete in postseason all-star games to improve their stock among the pro scouts. Not McKie and Jones. They were two of the best players in college basketball.

 Aaron's Thoughts

I heard a lot of people saying Eddie and I were first-round draft picks. I tried not to think about the NBA Draft. I heard stories where players were supposed to get picked in the first round and ended up going in the second round or not even being drafted at all. I didn't want to get my hopes up too much. My goal was to play as hard as I could. I figured if we could win as much as possible, that would help not only me but Rick Brunson, Derrick Battie, William Cunningham, and everybody else. The farther you go in the NCAA

Tournament, the more attention your team gets from the media, NBA scouts, and coaches.

On the other hand, I figured if I did get drafted in the first round, that would really be something. I would be able to take care of my family. I've really struggled over the years. I didn't have a lot of things. I was lucky to have people like coach Chaney, John Hardnett, and Bill Ellerbee to help me through the rough times. But coach Chaney along with everybody else didn't allow me to complain about not having a lot of money or material things. They wanted me to work hard in the classroom and on the court.

I would have to say the hard work really benefited me. I wasn't a McDonald's All-American at Simon Gratz. I was just happy to get a scholarship. I never stopped working. I didn't receive a lot of national publicity, but after four years at Temple, I was really pleased with the way everything worked out.

I was happy for Eddie, too. We were all in Indianapolis the night of the NBA Draft. Eddie had his family there. I had my Aunt Rose, my mother [Pearl McKie], and sister [Sandy McKie]. John Hardnett also came out to the draft. Coach Chaney didn't make it, but I know he was watching at home. This was a big moment for Eddie and myself.

This was the first time I had ever been to the RCA Dome. I had heard a lot about the building. It was beautiful. The NBA had everything organized from beginning to end.

The draft was on national television [TNT]. They had a special room for interviews, which was well organized. I remember being really anxious at the time.

On draft night, Eddie and I pretty much knew we were going in the first round. It was a matter of where and what team. Eddie was a lottery pick. He went to the Lakers with the 10th pick. Eddie was in a special class. He was drafted along with guys like Glenn Robinson, Jason Kidd, Grant Hill, and Juwan Howard. Actually, Glenn Robinson was the No. 1 pick by the Milwaukee Bucks.

After Eddie got drafted, I couldn't wait for them to call my name. I was a little tired of waiting. I was supposed to go to New Jersey with the 14th pick, but they took Yinka Dare from George Washington. But I knew Portland liked me. P. J. Carlesimo was the head coach. He told me if I was there, Portland was going to take me. That's exactly what happened. They called my name. I went up to get my hat and shake David Stern's hand.

Then, I went to the green room for an interview. After that I went back to my family. They congratulated me on being a first-round pick.

At that point, I thought about Eddie and I being apart for the first time in four years. We had been through so much together. We used to play basketball all the time. Now, we were going in different directions.

It was kind of sad. But coach Chaney prepares you for the next stage in life. Eddie and I have been friends for a long time. I knew I wouldn't be around him every day. We did a lot of talking about coach Chaney. We talked about all the times he hollered at us in practice. We talked about how we used to tease him on occasion. Moreover, we just remembered how he put us in this position.

People don't really know how good a coach he is. All the NBA scouts and coaches know him. They know if they get a Temple player, they're getting somebody who knows how to play the game. We're not going to embarrass the organization. We're going to win and do the right things. That's what coach Chaney taught us.

But I think to have Eddie and myself go in the first round is really a tribute to him. He doesn't get a lot of All-Americans. I know he had Mark Macon, Donald Hodge, and Rick Brunson. And I think he had a few others that were McDonald's All Americans [Mark Karcher and Kevin Lyde]. But that's not a lot of players. I mean, you have schools like North Carolina, Duke, and Kentucky. They get the cream of the crop. Coach has been there a long time [21 years]. During that time coach Chaney has taken a lot of kids and made them better players and better human beings.

That's what he's done with Eddie and myself. He's made us better players and better people.

 ## Eddie's Thoughts

I was really excited the night of the draft. I was a little nervous, too. I wanted them to hurry up and call my name. I know Aaron felt the same way. You're just sitting there waiting for David Stern to call your name. My mom, stepfather, and brothers were with me. You look around the RCA Dome and see all those great players like Glenn Robinson, Grant Hill, and Jason Kidd.

It's amazing to think that you've come this far. And to think Temple had two players taken in the first round. That's really a big achievement for everybody. I don't think there were too many schools that had more than one player drafted from the same team. I think California [Jason Kidd and Lamond Murray] and Michigan [Juwan Howard and Jalen Rose] may have been the only other schools [also Louisville, with Clifford Rozier and Greg Minor]. So that put Temple and coach Chaney in good company. Of course, coach Chaney didn't talk too much about Aaron and me being first-round picks. Obviously, he was happy for us. But I think coach Chaney wanted everything to work out for everybody. I'm sure he probably shed a few tears. He knows how hard Aaron and I worked to get to this level.

At any rate, I was very happy when the Lakers selected me. I used to watch them play against the Philadelphia 76ers and the Boston Celtics in the eighties. I thought it was a good situation for me. I was going to a winning team. I was already used to playing on winning teams at Temple.

Now I'm playing for the Miami Heat. But I was very happy being a first-round pick. This meant getting a nice contract and providing for my mother. She kept me on the right path. After my father died, she sat down and talked to me on several occasions about doing things that would make him proud. It's little things like that you don't forget. Aaron is pretty much the same way.

After David Stern announced my name, I waited for him to say Aaron McKie will be going to whatever team. I had to wait a few picks. Then, they announced that the Portland Trail Blazers' pick was Aaron McKie. A big smile came across my face.

The other thing that crossed my mind was Aaron and I had come quite a ways together. Now, we were going to be playing against each other. We were on the same team for three years. The only time we played against each other was in the Sonny Hill College League. We also played one-on-one in McGonigle Hall and Pearson Hall. This was definitely a new beginning for both of us.

CHAPTER 8

Rookie Year

The 1994–95 NBA season was McKie's and Jones' first year away from John Chaney and the Temple basketball program. That season, they spent a great deal of time on the phone talking to each other. McKie often gave Jones a call after a game to let him know how he had done. Jones did the same thing.

They also stayed in touch with Chaney and his team. Chaney frequently watched McKie and Jones play on television (he owns a satellite dish). He would stay up until almost 2:00 A.M. watching them play. Then, he would hold Temple basketball practice at 5:30 A.M. and talk about Aaron and/or Eddie.

Jones had a terrific rookie season. He was named to the NBA All-Rookie First Team after averaging 14.0 points, 3.9 rebounds, and 2.05 steals. He was named MVP of the Schick Rookie Game during the NBA All-Star Weekend in Phoenix, posting a game-high 25 points, six steals, and four rebounds. If Jones hadn't broken his hand and missed 18 games, he may have won the league's Rookie of the Year Award. Jones helped the Lakers secure a spot in the NBA Playoffs.

Although Jones didn't play a run-and-gun style at Temple, he was able to fit right in with the Lakers' fast-break offense.

He scored a career-high 31 points in only his fourth NBA game, against the Minnesota Timberwolves.

Jones led all NBA rookies in steals and ranked sixth overall in the league. He owned the NBA's best steal-to-turnover ratio (1.75), becoming the first rookie in NBA history to lead the league in that category.

McKie started 20 games as a rookie and scored in double figures in 14 of his final 26 games. He recorded career highs in field goals made (10), offensive rebounds (4), total rebounds (10), and points (20) in Portland's 99–90 victory over Miami on March 9. McKie's points and rebounds in that outing represented the first 20-10 game by a Portland rookie since Sam Bowie's 20-point, 15-rebound performance on March 10, 1985.

After seeing action in just 19 of Portland's first 56 games (averaging 2.0 points, 9.0 minutes), Aaron played in 34 of the Trail Blazers' final 37 games. He missed 27 games due to injury (a sprained right thumb and sprained right shoulder). Overall, he averaged 6.5 points, 2.9 rebounds, and 2.0 assists a game while helping the Trail Blazers make the playoffs.

Mark Macon, Temple's all-time leading scorer, was very impressed with the way both players handled themselves in their first season. In 1991 Macon had been drafted by the Denver Nuggets with the eighth pick in the first round. He played two seasons with the Nuggets and three with the Detroit Pistons.

"I thought Aaron and Eddie handled the pressure of being first-round picks very well," Macon said. "Everybody expects first-round picks to do something right away. I thought both of them made some nice contributions. It wasn't surprising to me. They've both been tested. I remember playing against them as freshmen. I used to play one-on-one full court against Aaron and Eddie. I really killed them the first year. After I came back from Denver the next year, they were killing me.

"Aaron and Eddie have survived the hard times. They've never let unfortunate incidents stop them from being successful. They're both good examples for the young players in coach Chaney's program."

The NBA lifestyle is glamorous. The teams fly around in chartered planes that have everything from soup to nuts. They stay in five-star hotels. They make a lot of money. The teams are constantly seen on national television.

This was a major adjustment for McKie and Jones. The travel schedule is grueling. One night you're in one place, the next day you're hundreds of miles away. That's not easy to get used to for most people.

When McKie and Jones weren't playing for their teams, they followed the Owls. They were particularly interested in Rick Brunson, Temple's backcourt ace, who now plays for the Chicago Bulls. Brunson, a 6'4" guard, had played three years with McKie and Jones.

Brunson led the Owls to the NCAA Tournament in 1995 for the sixth consecutive year. Temple finished at 19–11, 10–6 in the Atlantic 10 Conference, en route to qualifying for the A-10 championship game for the third straight season.

In the first round of the NCAA Tournament, freshman guard Johnny Miller, who would later transfer to Clemson, hit nine three-pointers and scored 30 points, but Temple fell to Cincinnati 77–71.

The young Owls got off to a 6–1 start in 1994–95. They slipped to 9–7 and needed a late charge to get into the tournament. Brunson provided that leadership. He led the Owls in every offensive category. Temple's five-game winning streak included victories over Louisville and Penn.

At George Washington, Brunson exploded for what was then a conference- and Temple-record nine three-pointers and scored 36 points.

"I used to tell the young guys about Aaron and Eddie," Brunson said. "I told them how they used to take over games. They would listen to me and shake their heads. Aaron and Eddie used to call all the time to see how we we're doing. I remember telling them, 'Don't worry. We'll be in the NCAA Tournament.' I told them that after we beat UMass at McGonigle Hall. I tease Marcus Camby [former Knicks teammate] about that game. I think Aaron and Eddie missed coach Chaney, the players, the students, and Temple."

The Temple basketball program has a family atmosphere because of coach Chaney. Aaron and Eddie used to keep in touch during their rookie year.

 ## Aaron's Thoughts

I tried to stay in contact with everybody. I would call coach Chaney during the day. I tried to reach him at the office. I usually called after practice. It would be early on the West Coast, but that didn't bother me. I was used to getting up early in the morning for coach Chaney's practices. If Coach wasn't around, I would talk to Ms. Davis. I would let her know what's going on. Then, I would ask her to have coach Chaney call me.

Basically, I just wanted to know how everything was going for him and the team. The NBA lifestyle is a major adjustment. Everybody used to say, "How can you get up at 5:30 in the morning for practice?" I used to tell them it didn't bother me. You get used to it after a while.

It was hard for me to get used to playing in Denver one night, then playing in Phoenix the next night. You're in and out of hotels and airports. I did some traveling at Temple, but we played in the Atlantic 10 Conference. Quite naturally, all the schools were in the East. I didn't have a problem going from Philly to Pittsburgh to play Duquesne. That was easy for me.

I had to keep up with what was going on back home. I tried to catch some of the Temple highlights on *SportsCenter*. We didn't have any of the Philly newspapers. That's why I had to call Coach, John Hardnett, or Eddie.

Eddie and I called each other on a regular basis. We would talk about the different players in the NBA. He would tell me how he made out against a certain opponent. I would tell him how I did against this player. Then, we used to get together whenever Portland played L.A.

It was nice coming home to play the Sixers my rookie year. I had a chance to see a lot of my friends from high school and college. I didn't get a chance to see coach Chaney. He may have been at the Final Four. I can't remember exactly. I really enjoy playing for the Sixers now. I know Coach was happy when Portland drafted me. I think coach Chaney feels it's better for local players to play away from home. I know he felt that way about Tim Perry, who used to play for the Sixers. It feels good to me. I don't have any problems playing at home.

The thing I missed the most about coach Chaney was his teaching and his stories. The NBA coaches assume you know everything, except for people like Larry

Brown. Coach Brown thoroughly explains his philosophy. That's the same way coach Chaney does in practices. He does such a good job of breaking everything down, I don't think anybody is in the dark. The matchup zone is the toughest thing to learn, but coach Chaney shows exactly how to play it. He may say something like, "You better move your big feet." And that's just to get you moving on the matchup. The man can coach and make you laugh at the same time.

The only thing, don't let him see you laughing. He may reach and grab you by the collar.

There's one other thing I learned from coach Chaney and Temple, and that's how to conduct yourself on the road. He didn't put up with a lot of foolishness. When you went someplace, he expected you to act like a gentleman. He didn't want to hear any bad reports about his players misbehaving or whatever. That's something I took with me to the NBA.

 ## Eddie's Thoughts

I didn't like calling coach Chaney too much. I didn't want to be a burden. He had his own players to worry about. They struggled a little bit my rookie year. But I told Coach not to worry about things; Rick Brunson will take care of everything. Rick was the most experienced player on the team. He got them to the [NCAA] Tournament, too.

I used to call Coach late at night sometimes. I know he stays up and watches television. Coach likes to joke around on the phone. I would call him and say, "Coach, are you awake?" He would say, "Who's this? Eddie? Eddie who?" Then, I would say, "Come on, Coach, stop playing games. You got a couple more hours before practice starts." You can't help but miss a guy like him. You're around him for four years.

I missed Aaron, too. We called each other as much as possible. He would fill me in on what was happening with the team. He would call me if they were on national television. That was the only way I would see Temple play. Whenever Temple played Cincinnati, Nick Van Exel [a former Laker] wanted to bet me. I remember Tony Smith [also a former Laker] used to tease me. He would say, "Temple's not that good." I told him they beat Marquette. That was Tony's school.

I always tried to do a good job of representing my school. I figured that would only help coach Chaney in terms of building the Temple program. After all, he gave me a chance to succeed at this level.

I was fortunate to play well in the Rookie Game. We made the playoffs my first year. Aaron helped the Trail Blazers get to the playoffs, too.

We were lucky to be a part of winning organizations. The Lakers and the Trail Blazers know what it's like to win. I'm saying that even now that I got traded. They have a foundation out there. They have a good tradition. It's just like Temple in some respects. Coach has built a winning program. Winning is a way of life. Or, like Coach says, "Winning is an attitude."

I had a lot of fun my rookie year. But I was glad when the season was over. This gave me a chance to come back to Philly. Aaron and I got together during the summer to play in the Baker League [a summer

85

league for the pros]. We worked out with all the Temple players during John Hardnett and Fred Douglas' workouts. We would come down to coach Chaney's office. He would ask us who was playing well. It was just like old times being back in McGonigle Hall. Aaron and I had been across the country playing in the biggest and finest arenas. After a year away or seven months away, it was nice to come home.

CHAPTER 9

Temple Is the Place for Chaney

J ohn Chaney is one of the most successful coaches in the history of college basketball. In fact, he has been a successful
junior high, high school, small college, and major college basketball coach. He was inducted into the Naismith Basketball Hall
of Fame in 2001.

The NBA is the only level of coaching Chaney hasn't tried
in his career. However, he did coach Kent's Taverneers to
five straight championships in the Charles Baker League, a
summer training ground for NBA, CBA, and professional players returning from abroad. Chaney coached and became a close
friend of 76ers Hal Greer, Chet Walker, and Ben Warley. Greer
and Walker started for the 76ers' 1966–67 NBA championship
team. Wilt Chamberlain, Wali Jones, Billy Cunningham, Luke
Jackson, and Bob Weiss played for other Baker League teams.
Chaney also coached Williamsport in the Eastern League from
1963 to 1966. He was an all-star point guard in the Eastern
League and Baker League before concentrating on coaching.

Of course, the early years of the Baker League and the
Eastern League were a different era of pro basketball. Players

didn't make as much money as they do today. They had a better appreciation for the game. The players were more dedicated to improving their game, and they showed a great deal of respect for the people involved with basketball—coaches, general managers, and fans.

At Sayre Junior High, Simon Gratz High School, the Baker League, and the Eastern League, Chaney coached man-to-man defense, and his teams ran and scored big numbers. His teams had good floor balance and took care of the ball, so it was easy to get back on defense.

At Cheyney, he inherited foul-prone big men, so at Temple he turned to good friends Jim Maloney and Jay Norman for zone lessons. Chaney adapts his matchup zone each season to suit the wills and skills of current players. His Owls press on man-to-man very well, for brief stints, usually in the second half.

Chaney is an old-fashioned guy. He doesn't go for a lot of flash and dash. He's a man who has certainly paid his dues. He and his wife, Jeanne, are the parents of a daughter (Pamela) and two sons (John and Darryl) and have four grandchildren.

He has been working for 43 years, including 17 years teaching and coaching in the Philadelphia Public School System, a decade teaching and coaching at Cheyney University, and 21 years as head coach at Temple.

He could walk away from coaching at any time. McKie and Jones are lucky Chaney didn't retire before they came to Temple. He's a man who obviously is not getting any younger.

The coaching profession is a tough grind. Today every kid thinks he's the next Michael Jordan or Kobe Bryant. Many of them want to leap from high school to the NBA. Others who do go to college want to leave after a year or two.

The NCAA continues to tighten the academic standards, making it harder and harder for marginal student-athletes to be eligible as freshmen. Then, there are the AAU (Amateur Athletic Union) coaches who organize traveling high school all-star teams. The coaches take some of the country's best high school players to different tournaments, where they play before a lot of major colleges. These coaches wield a lot of power, which can make recruiting a nightmare.

Coaches are crisscrossing the country to find the best players. On top of all this madness, there's an enormous amount of pressure to win games. Most coaches are measured by how many trips they make to the NCAA Tournament. If you haven't been to postseason play by your fourth season, more than likely you'll be out of a job. Chaney has been to the NCAA Tournament 17 times in his 21 years as Temple's coach. He doesn't have to worry about job security.

Chaney has built a magnificent basketball program. They have one of the winningest programs in the history of college basketball. Temple's name is right there with teams such as Kentucky, North Carolina, Kansas, Duke, and St. John's in regards to overall victories. The school has more than 1,600 wins. This success is largely because of Chaney.

It's hard to believe Chaney wouldn't be a successful coach in the NBA. A lot of coaches have gone from college to pro basketball. Some have done quite well. Others have really struggled.

After Chaney's first day in his Temple office in 1982, he relaxed at a Baker League game, where dozens of friends and admirers congratulated him.

One sportswriter said, "I know you will win a lot at Temple. If the 76ers ask you to rescue them in a few years, what will you say?"

Chaney replied, "Five years ago, it would have been very interesting, but it's too late. I have a great opportunity here at Temple, and I hope to be here a long time. How would I coach Darryl Dawkins? With a baseball bat."

Chaney usually was chosen to coach the Baker League All-Stars when they faced New York's pros, so he coached Wilt Chamberlain, Earl Monroe, Billy Cunningham, Ray "Chink" Scott, Tom "Trooper" Washington, and Bill Bradley, as well as Kent's Taverneers' Hal Greer and Chet Walker.

McKie and Jones feel Chaney is one of the greatest coaches in the game. But they both feel the NBA would not be a good situation for Chaney.

 **Eddie's Thoughts**

I don't think Coach could make it in the NBA. He's going to demand respect. That's just how he is. If a player didn't do something, I think coach Chaney would get very upset. You need a lot of patience to coach in the NBA. These guys make a lot of money. Some of them aren't as dedicated as others. If we had a Temple team in the NBA, Coach could handle them. If he had me, Aaron, Tim Perry, Mark Macon, Mark Strickland, Duane Causwell, and Rick Brunson, he would be all right.

I think some of these guys have been spoiled throughout their careers. They've had the best of everything. Well, nobody gets spoiled in the Temple program. I don't think coach Chaney could deal with guys with big egos. He would have a big problem with someone who thought he was really special.

You see, Coach taught me discipline. I don't think all the coaches across the country emphasize that. Coach Chaney also taught me character, responsibility, and other things. But you can see where some guys just played basketball in college. They didn't learn about life. They didn't have lectures at 5:30 A.M. like I did.

So, you're dealing with all kinds of personalities. Plus, there's a lot of politics in the NBA. You have a lot of people telling [coaches] what to do. Coach is not going to go for that. He runs the Temple basketball program.

I can picture Coach trying to get rid of somebody. I can hear him say, "This guy doesn't want to listen. We've got to move him." Then, the general manager says, "We can't trade him now." Coach would say, "Until you can trade him, he can't play for me."

There are some guys who could play for coach Chaney whether he was coaching in college or the pros. I think coach Chaney would like Derek Harper [former NBA guard]. Derek has a good understanding of the game. He listens, works hard, doesn't give anybody a hard way to go, and loves the game. He doesn't mess around, either. Coach would like that part. Derek was my teammate with the Lakers. He would have been a good Temple player, too.

I've never played with him, but I think Charles Oakley [Washington Wizards] could play for coach Chaney. I know Oakley's a rough player, but coach Chaney would like his work ethic. He goes after every rebound and loose ball. He plays good defense. He's not going to back down from a challenge.

There are other players in the league like them. We have some great players with Miami. I really like the players on our team. It's just that I've been in the league for nine years. I've seen how some players carry themselves on and off the court. You can tell some of them have been able to pretty much do whatever they want.

I just think for a guy like coach Chaney, Temple is the best place. He knows how the ground lays every year. He helps a lot of people like myself. He has a great basketball mind. He knows how to work with limited talent. He's a proven winner. I think sometimes it's best to stay in that situation.

On the other hand, it's really a shame. I believe a lot of NBA players could definitely learn from him. I think coaches like Paul Silas, Del Harris, Pat Riley, and Larry Brown know the value of having a Temple player on their team. They can see all the hard work coach Chaney has put in over the years.

Aaron's Thoughts

Coach Chaney wouldn't be happy in the NBA. It's not the same game as college basketball. We [76ers] had our training camp at the Liacouras Center, so coach Chaney would just walk over to our practices from his office. I remember we got a little sloppy with the ball. We threw it away a few times. Coach walked up to me after the practice and said, "You guys turn the ball over too much." I told him, "This is the NBA. The game is a little more wide-open. Guys are going to try to

Temple head coach John Chaney provides instruction during a game.
PHOTO COURTESY OF TEMPLE SPORTS.

Chaney with Aaron McKie during a game.
PHOTO BY ZOHRAB KAZANJIAN.

Eddie Jones (left), Aaron McKie (center), and coach Chaney (right) face the news media during a postgame press conference following an NCAA Tournament game.

PHOTO BY ZOHRAB KAZANJIAN.

Eddie Jones (second from left), Rick Brunson (third from left), and Aaron McKie (far right) accept a plaque from former Atlantic 10 Conference Commissioner Ron Bertovich (second from right) at the Atlantic 10 Conference Tournament.

PHOTO BY ZOHRAB KAZANJIAN.

Chaney watches the action from the sidelines with former assistant Dean Demopoulos.   PHOTO BY RODNEY ADAMS.

Aaron McKie prepares to make a pass to a teammate. McKie was named Atlantic 10 Conference Player of the Year in 1993. PHOTO COURTESY OF TEMPLE SPORTS.

Eddie Jones handles the ball for the Temple Owls. Jones was named Atlantic 10 Conference Player of the Year in 1994. PHOTO COURTESY OF TEMPLE SPORTS.

Aaron McKie shakes hands with NBA Commissioner David Stern during the NBA Draft. McKie was a first-round pick of the Portland Trail Blazers.

Eddie Jones pictured with Stern on draft night at the RCA Dome in Indianapolis. Jones was a first-round pick of the Los Angeles Lakers.

Aaron McKie (left) won the NBA's Sixth Man Award during the 2001 season. McKie is shown with Most Valuable Player Allen Iverson, Defensive Player of the Year Dikembe Mutombo, and Coach of the Year Larry Brown. McKie helped to lead the Sixers to the NBA Finals that year.

PHOTO COURTESY OF AP/WIDE WORLD PHOTOS.

McKie (left), now with the 76ers, tries to steal the ball from Detroit's Jon Barry during a game in Philadelphia in January of 2003.

PHOTO COURTESY OF AP/WIDE WORLD PHOTOS.

Jones, now a high-scoring guard with the Miami Heat, takes a shot over Philadelphia 76ers guard Eric Snow. PHOTO COURTESY OF AP/WIDE WORLD PHOTOS.

make a few more plays on their own." Then coach Chaney said, "You've got to protect the ball."

Hey, I know what coach Chaney was talking about. He doesn't like to see the ball turned over. Turnovers are not permitted in the Temple program. I know that would drive him crazy. In the NBA, players do take more chances with the ball. Consequently, there's going to be more turnovers. I know Larry Brown doesn't like a lot of turnovers. That's one reason why we got along so well.

I couldn't see him leaving Philadelphia. This is home for him. I can't see him coaching the Dallas Mavericks.

I think some college coaches try to come up to this level for money and prestige. Coach isn't about that. He's not looking for a $10-million-a-year contract to coach in the NBA. He doesn't do things for publicity. He's not seeking anything.

I'm not sure how coach Chaney would deal with some of the personalities in this league. The NBA has some great people. My teammates are good people. But there are some guys who are not the easiest people to contend with on a daily basis. I've played for three teams in this league. Every situation is different.

I just think he wouldn't tolerate any foolishness. He's an old-school guy. He would tell these players right up front what he expected from them. It would be either his way or the highway. You can't trade everybody in the NBA. Some guys are hard to trade because of their contract. That would just frustrate him even more.

I think coach Chaney likes the game. I know he watches a lot of basketball on television. He knows more than enough basketball to easily coach in the

NBA. Actually, he probably knows more than most guys who have coached in this league.

But I think he's more valuable at a place like Temple. He can do more things there. He can save lives there. The NBA is a business. Coach Chaney knows how to take care of business. The only thing he's in the business of is helping people. Coach Chaney isn't interested in making a lot of money. He could walk away from the game right now. And one day, that's going to happen. But I couldn't see him at any other place than Temple University. That may sound a little selfish. It's just that he's helped me and so many people throughout his career.

CHAPTER 10

Giving Back

Mckie and Jones realized how fortunate they were long before they became professional basketball players. They look back at their childhood and see that if it weren't for certain people, they could have easily gone in the wrong direction. Eddie credits his mother for keeping him on the path to success. Aaron can point to such people as Bill Ellerbee and John Hardnett.

McKie and Jones are now in positions where they can make a difference in the lives of many young people. They remember and appreciate all the people who helped them over the years. Moreover, they remember all the support Chaney gave them throughout their Temple careers. Since then, McKie and Jones—along with Mark Macon, Tim Perry, Mark Strickland, and Duane Causwell—bought a suite in honor of Chaney when the Liacouras Center (originally named The Apollo of Temple) was built five years ago.

McKie and Jones have also established the John Chaney Sr. Endowed Scholarship Fund for needy students.

They have learned the importance of helping others from being around Chaney. Every year, Chaney and Sonny Hill hold a basketball camp for two weeks at Temple's Ambler campus, providing many inner-city kids like them with a chance to learn basketball. They know that Chaney does many speaking engagements and clinics for free. More than that, Chaney has given some much needed fatherly advice to so many players.

McKie and Jones are now in positions where they can make a difference in the lives of young people. They can walk down Broad Street just a few blocks from the Temple campus in the pouring rain and put up an umbrella to keep the youngsters dry while giving them a lift home. This may not sound like much to most people, but for many inner-city kids that means a lot.

Aaron and Eddie know Chaney has been helping youngsters for more than 30 years. He knows that kids from poor families need an education in order to compete for a job. The late Al McGuire, former Marquette basketball coach and college basketball announcer for CBS, didn't want Chaney to retire.

"John, please don't leave," McGuire said during a Temple broadcast. "Come back and save another four kids."

McGuire realized there aren't a lot of coaches like Chaney left in the game—coaches who aren't interested in making a lot of money and are concerned only with helping kids.

McKie and Jones were two of the four kids Chaney saved every year. Chaney has watched them grow over the years as great basketball players, students, and young men. The growth is similar to the way a father looks at his sons once they reach a certain age. Chaney knows why McKie and Jones have become successful.

"They didn't come to Temple with all the answers," Chaney said. "Aaron and Eddie listened every day. They listened to the right people. Listening is very important. They had a lot to overcome in their lives. They couldn't have done it without help. What makes me feel good is they always came back to the people who helped them along the way. That shows me they really care."

Chaney's efforts have made lasting impressions on both players. McKie and Jones realize there aren't many John Chaneys in the world. They still see a lot of kids growing up without mothers and/or fathers. They read the newspapers and see the violence affecting youngsters in urban areas as well as in suburban neighborhoods.

McKie and Jones won't forget the bridge that carried them over. They have plans for once the balls stop bouncing and their NBA careers come to a screeching halt. They will continue to take care of their families. They will continue to support the Temple basketball program, even long after Chaney is gone. McKie and Jones have endured quite a bit themselves. They have also learned a great deal through education and personal experiences.

 ## Aaron's Thoughts

I was a social work major at Temple. I had two internships my senior year. The first one was an after-school program at a church near 8th and Diamond Streets. I lived with my Aunt Rose not too far from there. Most of the kids were from North Philly. Like me, they didn't have a lot of resources. I worked with kids from grades five through eight. I would help them with their homework. I would spend time talking to them about life.

The kids used to ask me about playing for coach Chaney. They all know I played basketball for Temple. They used to ask, "Why is he so mean?" They would see Coach on television hollering at the officials after a bad call. I told them he's tough. He's very demanding. He wants you to do well. In doing so, he may be a little hard on you. But coach Chaney really cares about his players. I really enjoyed working with the kids. They need somebody who cares about them. This is a quality I got from coach Chaney and the Sonny Hill League program. I've seen coach Chaney, John Hardnett, and Herm Rogul do things for no pay. They're about helping people. That's the way I am, too.

Right now, I'm taking care of everybody. I'm helping out my mother [Pearl], my sister [Jackie], my nephews [Khari and Shaun], and my daughter, Erin. I want to make things all right for everybody.

That's how people were with me. Especially those who were very close to me. They did a lot of things for me. This could be anything from tickets to a basketball game to giving me a ride.

I know having people take an interest in me was very important. This wasn't my only internship. I had one at Ben Franklin High School. I worked with students in 10th, 11th, and 12th grade. I had to go down to the school four times a week. I would go down after practice. I worked with students who once again didn't have a lot of money. Of course, these students were a lot older. But they also had a lot of problems. Some of them had no electricity, gas, or water at home. Part of my job was to connect them with community agencies that provide social services.

It was a good experience for me. It told me how fortunate I was to have these things. The other thing I did was talk to them about life and how to survive. I tried to tell them to never give up hope and believe in themselves. The internship was really hard sometimes. I mean, I would go back to my dorm and just shake my head.

I decided then that I wanted to get involved in social work. I still feel that way now. I'm playing for the Sixers right now. But one day, my career is going to be over. Life after basketball for me will be working with young people. I may have my own nonprofit organization. I may be working for someone else. But I'll certainly have some involvement with the community.

Eddie's Thoughts

I come back every summer and share my experiences with the different players on coach Chaney's team. I usually see them at John Hardnett's workouts. I know Coach has told them about Aaron and myself. I don't know the players that well. But I like them to see me.

I want them to know that I came through the same program as them. It is certainly a way of reaching back. Mark Macon really helped Aaron, Rick [Brunson], and myself. He inspired us to play as hard as we could.

I know coach Chaney likes that we come back to Temple. I enjoy coming back during the summer. Sometimes I don't have time to stop there during the NBA season. I think Rick is a little better at that than I am.

But coach Chaney is a very giving person. He didn't have things easy coming up as a young man. Everybody knows he's worked hard to be one of the best coaches in college basketball. He had to go through a lot more than we did to get where he is today.

That's why he's tried to pave the way for a lot of kids. He knows that it's very difficult to succeed without an education. Actually, him bringing players to his program is one of his ways of reaching back. Coach knows that if somebody didn't take an interest in him, there's a good chance he would have struggled through life.

He believes once you've had a certain level of success, you should share that with others. You don't have to be a professional basketball player to do that. If you know coach Chaney, he's not trying to send guys to the NBA. He's giving them a chance to receive education through playing basketball.

I'm trying to use basketball to help kids, too. I've started the Eddie Jones Foundation for Underprivileged Kids. The foundation encourages kids to do well on and off the court. You have to work hard in the classroom to be able to take advantage of the various activities organized by the foundation. We give money to the YMCA, the AAU, and the Sonny Hill League.

I'm really happy to be one of the Sonny Hill League sponsors. I know Sonny Hill from my days at Temple. I've seen what his league has done for so many people throughout the city. I played in his College League. I know a lot of the people associated with the program are about helping kids.

The foundation does some other things, too. I have a free basketball camp at my old high school [Ely] in Pompano Beach [Florida]. I have a camp in Los Angeles for kids. The foundation also takes them on trips in the summer. In the future, I hope to do some clinics in Philadelphia. I think the big thing with my foundation is helping kids. I know coach Chaney has reached out to a lot of athletes from poor families. He's given them an opportunity to play basketball and go to college.

I want to take that same concept. I want to help kids, too. I'm just doing it at a younger age. It's important to give kids something to do today. If not, they can very easily get into trouble. You don't want them to have too much time on their hands. Basketball is something most kids enjoy doing.

The foundation is something I wanted to do since I became a professional basketball player. I want to continue to help kids for a long time. You see a person like coach Chaney who has helped people for years, and it just makes you want to do more.

Coach Chaney has been giving kids a chance to achieve for over 30 years. It will take me a long time to catch up to him. After he retires from coaching, he'll probably continue to do favors, write letters, and make phone calls to help people who need a chance.

The only way I could catch up to coach Chaney would be for him to stop and do nothing for about 10 years. I only plan to play another seven years in the NBA. That means I'll be ready to retire at the end of my next contract. I'll be in my thirties. I know guys hang around until they're 38 or 40 years old. They can make a good living and that's fine. But I'll be prepared to do something else. More than likely, I'll continue to build my foundation. I want to help as many people as possible.

Afterword

The bright lights are on. The producer counts down: "four, three, two, one . . . roll 'em." John Chaney is sitting about five feet from Vivica A. Fox, one of the prettiest women in Hollywood. Fox has starred in several movies, such as *Independence Day*, *Set It Off*, *Two Can Play That Game*, and *Soul Food*.

She was hired by Host Communications, a sports production company based in Louisville, Kentucky, to interview Chaney for a nationally syndicated documentary. Fox asked Chaney a series of questions about his career. While most men would have been mesmerized by her beauty, Chaney sat there and answered questions regarding Bobby Knight, early-morning practices, and growing up.

Each question was answered thoroughly. As the interview went on, Fox was not only learning more about Chaney, the school's Hall of Fame coach, but she was finding out more about him as a person.

"It's really an honor and a pleasure to interview you, coach Chaney," Fox said after the taping was completed.

Chaney has that way about him. He always tells you something new. Or something you didn't know. He has a great vision on life. He has been coaching and working with young people for more than 30 years.

During that time, Chaney has turned a number of fine players into great people. He has given many athletes a chance to better themselves. Chaney hopes that they will return to their neighborhoods and inspire others to go on to higher education.

Some of the kids who play for him come from broken families, where only one parent, or perhaps just a grandparent, try to raise a family. Chaney will continue to gravitate toward players like McKie and Jones. That may be his biggest legacy.

Several years ago, he recruited Ernest Pollard, an All-City performer at Philadelphia's Roman Catholic High School. Pollard was a Proposition 48 casualty. He lived on the rugged streets of North Philadelphia near the Temple campus. When Chaney was recruiting Pollard, he told Pollard's mother that her son would graduate from college. And that's exactly what Pollard did. Today, Pollard is a terrific role model for many kids in his community. He is a member of the Philadelphia Police Department. He's also the director of the North Penn Police Athletic League Center in North Philadelphia.

Pollard didn't come from a wealthy family. However, his basketball scholarship allowed him to find the path to success.

Now, because of Pollard, other kids can dream. Chaney believes in dreams.

The next Aaron McKie, Eddie Jones, or Ernest Pollard is Alex Wesby, another kid from North Philly. Wesby, like Chaney, graduated from Ben Franklin High School. He was also Public League Player of the Year, just as Chaney was during his scholastic career. But Chaney couldn't play for Temple or any Big 5 school at that time because they weren't taking black players. So, he went to Bethune-Cookman, a historically black college in Daytona Beach, Florida. He became an NAIA All-American in college.

However, he couldn't play in the NBA because the league didn't allow blacks during the fifties. He spent 10 years playing in the Eastern League, where he was a seven-time All-Star and a two-time MVP.

After his playing career, he started coaching at Philadelphia's Sayre Junior High School and then Simon Gratz High School. In 1972 Chaney became the head basketball coach at Cheyney State. He had a marvelous coaching career there, posting a 225–59 record. This also included a 1978 NCAA Division II championship.

In spite of his success, Chaney didn't get an opportunity to coach major college basketball until the age of 50. He knows what it's like to be denied an opportunity. He's been there.

He doesn't want to see that happen to his players. Chaney doesn't believe in squashing dreams or limiting access and opportunity for youngsters.

Wesby, a sport- and recreation-management major, fell prey to Proposition 48. He wasn't able to compete his first season. But Wesby didn't let that stop him. He has received an extra year of eligibility thanks to his hard work in the classroom. He has also graduated with his degree in tourism and hospitality. At 6'6", Wesby can hit from three-point range, glide to the basket, handle the ball, and play great defense. He could wind up in the NBA.

Under Chaney, Temple has developed quite a reputation for producing solid NBA players, such as McKie and Jones. But that's not important to Chaney. The most significant thing about Wesby is that he is the first person in his family to graduate from college. The college degree will carry him a lot further in life. For that alone, Wesby will be a better person.

Chaney remembers what he learned from Mary McLeod Bethune, the great black educator who founded Bethune-Cookman College, his alma mater.

"She used to say, 'As you rise, you must lift,'" Chaney said.

In other words, once you've received your education, you should help the next person achieve that goal.

"What I liked about the black schools is they never put a ceiling on what you could learn," Chaney said. "They believed in building up the floor so that you could reach all ceilings. They never said that there's a score that says you can't do it. They believed in access and opportunity. They gave me that chance."

Chaney's memory is long. He doesn't forget the people who encouraged him throughout his career. One person he can never forget is his high school coach, Sam Browne, who provided him with the dream of going to college.

"He would not allow me to do anything but go to college," Chaney said. "He worked extremely hard to convince my parents that I should go to college.

"I remember in the summer he would find time to buy us clothes because we were very poor. He would take us out to the Poconos and the mountains so we could be free from all the gangs and other problems we had in the city. He convinced me I had an opportunity to go to school."

Chaney is a rare breed. They don't make them like him anymore. He stresses discipline with his players. He said in a recent interview that discipline is one of the highest forms of intelligence. Not many people are doing the things he does at Temple.

There has been a lot of talk over the past few years about him retiring. Only Chaney knows when he'll step down from coaching. The one thing that's certain is that the school will really miss him.

Appendix I

John Chaney's Coaching Record

John Chaney's Coaching Record

1972–73	Cheyney State	23–5	NCAA Division II Tournament
1973–74	Cheyney State	19–7	NCAA Division II Tournament
1974–75	Cheyney State	16–9	
1975–76	Cheyney State	24–5	NCAA Division II Tournament
1976–77	Cheyney State	20–8	NCAA Division II Tournament
1977–78	Cheyney State	27–2	NCAA Division II Tournament *(national champion)*
1978–79	Cheyney State	24–7	NCAA Division II Tournament *(third place)*
1979–80	Cheyney State	23–5	NCAA Division II Tournament
1980–81	Cheyney State	21–8	NCAA Division II Tournament
1981–82	Cheyney State	28–3	NCAA Division II Tournament
1982–83	Temple University	14–15	
1983–84	Temple University	26–5	NCAA Tournament *(second round)*
1984–85	Temple University	25–6	NCAA Tournament *(second round)*
1985–86	Temple University	25–6	NCAA Tournament *(second round)*

1986–87	Temple University	32–4	NCAA Tournament *(second round)*
1987–88	Temple University	32–2	NCAA Tournament *(East Regional Finals)*
1988–89	Temple University	18–12	National Invitation Tournament
1989–90	Temple University	20–11	NCAA Tournament
1990–91	Temple University	24–13	NCAA Tournament *(East Regional Finals)*
1991–92	Temple University	17–13	NCAA Tournament
1992–93	Temple University	20–13	NCAA Tournament *(West Regional Finals)*
1993–94	Temple University	23–8	NCAA Tournament *(second round)*
1994–95	Temple University	19–11	NCAA Tournament
1995–96	Temple University	20–13	NCAA Tournament *(second round)*
1996–97	Temple University	20–11	NCAA Tournament *(second round)*
1997–98	Temple University	21–9	NCAA Tournament
1998–99	Temple University	24–11	NCAA Tournament *(East Regional Finals)*
1999–2000	Temple University	27–6	NCAA Tournament *(second round)*
2000–01	Temple University	24–13	NCAA Tournament *(South Regional Finals)*
2001–02	Temple University	19–15	National Invitation Tournament *(third place)*
2002–03	Temple University	18–16	National Invitation Tournament *(quarter finals)*

10-Year Cheyney Record: 225–59 (.792)

21-Year Temple Record: 468–210 (.690)

31-Year Overall Record: 693–269 (.720)

Appendix II
Newspaper Coverage of John Chaney's Career

Terence Stansbury
Pleases Pacers

THE *PHILADELPHIA TRIBUNE*, NOVEMBER 20, 1984

There are a lot of great rookies in the NBA this season—Hakeem Olajuwon, Michael Jordan, and Charles Barkley, just to name a few. Terence Stansbury, Temple's all-time leading scorer, has also been playing extremely well as a rookie with the Indiana Pacers.

Stansbury, a 6'5" guard, scored 25 points as Indiana shocked unbeaten Houston, 125–117, Wednesday [November 14, 1984].

"I'm gradually getting used to the NBA style of play," Terence said. "We've got some great players in this league. Every night you're going up against somebody who's an outstanding player. So far, I've been doing all right. I've had some pretty good shooting games. I just want to keep it going and help the team win."

Pacers head coach George Irvine believes Stansbury has all the skills to become a terrific pro.

"We're very pleased with his game," Irvine said. "We feel Terence is one of the best rookie guards in the league. He does so many great things on the court. He can shoot, pass, and

113

handle the ball very well. We're very fortunate to have a player of his caliber."

Stansbury was acquired by the Pacers in a late preseason deal that also brought them Bill Garnett from the Dallas Mavericks. The ex-Owl was the Mavericks second first-round draft pick. He was advised to hold out for a better contract by his agent Bill Pollak, but Stansbury signed on his own and joined the Mavericks camp in the middle of the preseason.

When he arrived he found himself behind rookie guards Tom Sluby and Howard Carter. Stansbury had to work extremely hard to get some playing time before the Mavericks sent him to the Pacers.

"I was a little surprised when they traded me," Terence said. "I thought they would give me a chance to get myself together. But I think things will work out for me. We've got a very young team with a lot of potential. We have some great players, like Clark Kellogg, Herb Williams, Tony Brown, and Vern Fleming. We're going to be all right. The only thing we're lacking is experience."

Indiana's color commentator, Dick Vitale, really enjoys watching Stansbury play.

"He's a fine player," Vitale said. "Terence is so smooth on the court. He makes jump shooting look easy. Defensively, you can tell right away that he played for John Chaney, because he's all over the court. He's only going to get better as the season goes on."

Stansbury keeps in touch with his friends on the Owls basketball team.

"I've talked with Charlie [Rayne], Kevin [Clifton], and Dwight [Forrester] a few times," he said. "I explained to them what was happening with me. I wanted to keep them informed as to how I was making out. I also wanted to hear about how the team was doing. I think they're going to do just fine this year. I keep telling coach Chaney and coach [Jay] Norman not to worry about a thing."

Stansbury is adjusting to Indianapolis.

"Hey, it's cold out there," he said. "I've got to buy some winter clothes pretty soon. The next time we come to Philly, I'm going to have a winter coat on."

Asked about fellow player Granger Hall, Stansbury said, "I think Granger can certainly play in the NBA. I know some people may question his physical status because of the injury, but he's one of the best players in the country."

Asked about the Baker League, he said, "I won't make this mistake [his agent advised him not to play] again. I'll definitely be playing in the Baker League this summer. And this will be my decision."

Brokenborough Shoots for Owls, Roots for U-City

THE *PHILADELPHIA TRIBUNE*, FEBRUARY 16, 1998

Rasheed Brokenborough knows what time of year it is. Brokenborough, a 6'4", 185-pound junior, has been focusing on getting the Temple Owls prepared for their annual drive to the Atlantic 10 Tournament and the NCAA Championship. However, the Owls' shooting guard is also keeping track of his alma mater, University City High School, in the Public League playoffs.

"I haven't been able to see any games this season," Brokenborough said. "I have been in touch with coach [Steve] Kane. He keeps me informed with how the team is doing on a regular basis. He's doing a good job. I hope they can go all the way."

Brokenborough played on the 1995 U-City team that defeated Simon Gratz for the league title. That was a special year for the Jaguars. The women's team, led by Shawnetta Stewart (who later played for Rutgers), won their championship as well.

"I'll never forget it," Brokenborough said. "Both teams winning championships—that was really something. It meant a lot to the students, staff, alumni, and the community. We had a number of celebrations recognizing the team. There's nothing like winning."

The Temple Owls have developed one of the finest winning traditions in college basketball. Brokenborough is familiar with the tradition. In fact, he's already a part of it. A year ago, he played a huge part in leading the Owls to a 20–11 season and a spot in the NCAA Tournament.

"I got a good taste of the NCAA Tournament," Brokenborough said. "We played Mississippi in the first round. Then we played Minnesota in the second round. I would like to go further in the tournament. I guess it's because so many people watch basketball during this time. Believe it or not, the conference tournaments are getting just as big."

The Atlantic 10 tourney will be held at the Spectrum from March 3–7 [1998]. The Owls should be right in the thick of things. Temple (with a 16–6 overall record, 9–3 in their league) has posted some impressive wins over Massachusetts and Rhode Island. But the Owls have also put together some lackluster performances against Fordham and Virginia Tech.

"We should be all right," said Brokenborough, who averages 12.5 points and 3.5 rebounds a game. "I have a lot of confidence in my teammates. I know coach [John] Chaney gets concerned with our play at times. But I know we're capable of meeting the challenge. The A-10 Tournament is one of the best in the country. Everybody raises their level of play at tournament time."

Greer and Kearse
Will Meet Again in Big Dance;
Owls Draw West Virginia in Opener

THE *PHILADELPHIA TRIBUNE*, MARCH 10, 1998

When Temple faces West Virginia in the first round of the NCAA Tournament on Thursday, March 12 [1998], Lynn Greer, former Engineering & Science star, will have a chance to renew an old rivalry with ex–Simon Gratz standout Jarrett Kearse.

Greer and Kearse, two of the Public League's finest basketball players, have played against each other in the playoffs the last two seasons [1996 and 1997]. A year ago, Engineering & Science lost to Simon Gratz in the league championship game. Two years ago, the Bulldogs defeated the Engineers in the league playoffs. Greer is hoping to turn the tables in the big dance.

"I'm 0-and-2 against Jarrett," Greer said. "Gratz always beats us in high school. I think it's great that Jarrett and I are in the NCAA playoffs. I know a lot of people will be watching us play. I'm looking forward to playing against him. I just hope we can win this time.

"Everybody watches college basketball in March. It's one of the best times of the year to be a fan. I'm really excited about going to the tournament. I've been in the Public League playoffs. But the NCAA Tournament is really special. I know that's how I feel."

John Chaney, Temple basketball coach, feels Greer has played some outstanding basketball for the Owls.

"I didn't expect Lynn to come in and play as well as he did," Chaney said. "He's only a freshman. I didn't want to put a lot of pressure on him or Quincy Wadley [sophomore]. But I think Lynn has responded very well. He's done a nice job of handling the ball and shooting from the outside. He made a lot of big shots for us."

Greer has been a terrific scorer throughout his playing career. At E&S he racked up a career total of 1,991 points, which placed him second behind 1955 Overbrook High and NBA legend Wilt Chamberlain, with 2,206 points.

This season he certainly didn't disappoint the Owls. The 6'2", 165-pound guard averaged 8.1 points a game while shooting 48 percent from the three-point range and 80 percent from the free throw line.

"I tried to give the team a lift whenever I came into the game," Greer said. "We have some great players like Rasheed [Brokenborough], Lamont [Barnes], Pepe [Sanchez], Lynard [Stewart], and Quincy. I just wanted to hit the open man, handle the ball, and play good defense. I tried to stay away from making a lot of mistakes. I know coach Chaney doesn't like turnovers. So I've tried to keep them down to a minimum."

Greer doesn't expect his mother, Alma, father, Lynn Sr., and sister, Kelli, to travel to Boise, Idaho, for the matchup between Temple (21–8) and West Virginia (22–8). However, Greer knows his family and friends will all gather around the television set.

"I don't think my family will go to Boise, Idaho," Greer said. "It's a little too far. I think if we were playing a little closer to home, they would probably be there. But I know they'll be watching on television. Hopefully, we can give them something to cheer about."

Wesby Will Take His Talent to Temple

THE *PHILADELPHIA TRIBUNE*, MAY 15, 1998

Alex Wesby, Ben Franklin High's Public League Player of the Year, will play his college basketball for the Temple Owls next year. Wesby, a 6'6" senior forward, selected Temple over Massachusetts, Tulane, and Siena.

"Temple is a good situation for me," Wesby said. "It's close to home. I'm already established here. The people in the news media know me from playing in the city. Academically, Temple offers computer technology as a course of study. I plan to major in computer science.

"They have a great basketball program. Coach [John] Chaney is a great man. He does a good job of preparing his players for the next level or the real world. I'm really excited about going there."

Wesby averaged 21.5 points and 10.1 rebounds a game while leading the Electrons to the league championship over Franklin Learning Center. He has played on winning teams throughout his scholastic career. Wesby is familiar with the Owls' winning tradition.

"I know Temple goes to the NCAA Tournament every year," Wesby said. "Everybody knows Temple as a tournament team. That was also a big consideration in my decision. The decision wasn't an easy one. I really liked UMass with Bruiser [James Flint], coach [Paul] Hewitt with Siena, and the coach with Tulane [Perry Clark]. They all have good teams. Once again, I just think Temple is the best place for me."

Wesby is currently a partial qualifier. He has done extremely well in all his classes. However he needs the required score of 820 on his SAT to be eligible to play during his freshman year.

"I'm taking a class to help me improve my score," Wesby said. "I want to play this year. If I can get the number, I'll be out there. I take the SAT again on June 6 [1998]. In the meantime, I'm going to work very hard to prepare myself for the test."

The Owls have been very successful in landing some of the Public League's top players, such as Lynn Greer, Malik Moore, and Rasheed Brokenborough. Wesby is very close to a number of current Temple players.

"I know Lynn, Malik, and Rasheed really well," Wesby said. "I played against Lynn in the Public League. I know Malik and Rasheed from the Sonny Hill League and watching them play for Temple. I'm looking forward to playing with them."

Before Wesby puts on his cherry and white uniform, he plans to attend several summer workouts with Sonny Hill League coaches John Hardnett and Fred Douglas. Wesby needs to sharpen his ball-handling and shooting skills against topflight competition.

"I'm going to be working out with Mr. Hardnett and Mr. Douglas," Wesby said. "I've got to work on my outside shot and dribbling. I want to play the three position. I know Mr. Hardnett and Mr. Douglas usually have workouts with Aaron McKie, Eddie Jones, and Theo Ratliff. These guys play in the NBA. They'll help me improve my game. I want to be ready when basketball season comes around."

Senor, Steal

THIS ARTICLE ORIGINALLY APPEARED IN THE
1999 BASKETBALL HALL OF FAME TIP-OFF CLASSIC PROGRAM

Juan "Pepe" Sanchez has stolen games and broken hearts throughout his entire career at Temple. But the quickest hands might belong to the Owls coaching staff that "stole" Sanchez away from his native Argentina four years ago. With Pepe stealing the show each night, Temple has positioned itself for a coveted run at the Final Four.

When college basketball rolls out the premier point guards this year, the list will be highlighted by Mateen Cleaves of Michigan State, James "Scoonie" Penn of Ohio State, and Ed Cota of North Carolina. Juan "Pepe" Sanchez, Temple's 6'4" senior guard, is one of college basketball's premier playmakers. His play compares to the best guards in the country even though his name might not be as recognizable.

Sanchez has been nothing short of sensational for the Owls. A year ago he averaged 7.8 points and 5.2 rebounds a game. He also tallied 150 assists and 73 steals last season. For his efforts, Sanchez earned first team All–Atlantic 10 Conference recognition.

"Pepe Sanchez does a lot of things for Temple," said St. Joseph head coach Phil Martelli. "He runs the offense extremely well. He looks for the open man. He's able to create his own shot when the offense breaks down. Pepe's a clutch player. He's not afraid to take the big shot. In addition to his basketball skills, the guy is a great leader."

Sanchez played a major role in leading the Owls to the Atlantic 10 Conference East Division, the conference tournament finals, and the NCAA Elite Eight. The Owls' backcourt ace is the team's most consistent player. On the court he does everything effortlessly.

"Pepe is a very intelligent player," said Temple coach John Chaney. "We count on him to make good decisions. His ability to see the entire floor is one of the reasons why he's so valuable to us. He plays the game with plenty of savvy. He's improved his game every year. We have a pretty young team. But we need a player like him on the floor because of his experience."

Speaking of experience, Sanchez, a native of Bahia Blanca, Argentina, played three seasons (1993–95) with the Argentina Junior National Team. In his first season the team won the Bolivian Tournament with seven consecutive wins. He was also named MVP of the tournament after averaging 10.6 points and 5.3 assists a game.

At the 1995 Pan-American Games his team finished second to the USA, falling to an American team led by Stephon Marbury (former Georgia Tech star who now plays for the New Jersey Nets) in the championship. In the next games his team finished sixth, but defeated the USA entry, which included Marbury and ex–Louisville standout Sumaki Walker. Sanchez led that competition with an average of 4.5 steals a game.

He next joined the Argentina "Under 22" competition level and led his team to the finals of the South American Tournament against Brazil. He played in the Pan-American Pre–World Championship Tournament in Puerto Rico in August 1996 and guided his team to a third-place finish.

"I think the experience really helped me," Sanchez said. "I played against a lot of great players before I came to Temple. When you play against good players, it's only going to raise the level of your game. I've tried to use my experience from playing for the Argentina Junior National Team to benefit our team."

Chaney learned about Sanchez's magnificent skills from George Severini, who used to coach in Argentina. Severini knew Chaney from his coaching days at Cheyney State. Chaney had also conducted several clinics in Argentina, and Severini coached some of Chaney's former players in Philadelphia's Charles Baker League.

Severini, who is now the head soccer coach at Haverford High School in Pennsylvania, saw Sanchez as a high school player. He called Chaney and told him about the gifted young athlete. Severini's recommendation provided the Owls with a terrific lead guard.

"I've known John Chaney for a long time," Severini said. "He used to do a lot of basketball clinics in Argentina. He became the most popular basketball coach in Argentina. Everybody loves him down there. I told him about Pepe a few years ago. A friend of mine had seen him play before I did. I saw that Pepe was a very talented player. I know John used to always ask me to send him a 6'10" or 7'0" center from Argentina. I couldn't do that. But I sent him some tapes of Pepe playing against some great players. Obviously, he liked what he saw on the tapes and offered him a scholarship.

"I go to see all of the Temple games. I'm really proud of Pepe. He's done very well at Temple. Moreover, I think he's playing for one of the best coaches in the country. I know Pepe can learn a great deal about basketball and life from him."

Sanchez certainly is the kind of playmaker who can control the game. It's something Chaney noticed right away.

"I was very impressed with his poise on the court," Chaney said. "He was a great passer and defensive player. He had the ability to hit the open shot. Pepe brought all those skills to our program. You can tell Pepe played a lot of basketball down there. He fits in very well. He's done all the things we've asked him to do. He's played very well for us each year. You can just look at the things he's done."

As a freshman, Sanchez was named to the A-10 All-Rookie team. He averaged 10 points a game while leading the Owls in both assists (5.3 per game, 163 total) and steals (2.8 per game, 86 total). In his sophomore year Sanchez was selected as the conference Defensive Player of the Year and made third team All-Conference. He is the first player under Chaney to turn a triple-double performance, scoring 10 points, grabbing 10 rebounds, and making 10 assists in an 80–66 victory over La Salle. Sanchez boosted his game another notch in his junior year. In addition to receiving All-Conference honors, he was named Big 5 Player of the Year.

This native of Argentina has grown to appreciate the Philadelphia basketball tradition. "The people in Philly really love basketball," Sanchez said. "You can see it by just going around the city. The Big 5 games have been very intense. Everybody wants to beat each other. It's been exciting for me. The games are usually very close."

Three years ago Sanchez found out exactly how close the Big 5 games can be when he hit a 40-foot three-pointer at the buzzer to beat La Salle, 70–67, in double overtime. Of course Sanchez eclipsed that performance by scoring nine of eleven points in the final 2:47 minutes, including two crucial free throws with a half second left, as Temple knocked off Michigan State, 60–59, in a battle between two of the nation's best teams.

"Pepe has been a clutch player throughout his career," said Quincy Wadley, Temple's 6'4" senior guard. "He's not afraid to take the big shot. He's pulled out some big games for us. He's a big reason why we've done so well over the years."

The Owls are expected to do well this year. Some college basketball experts believe they have a chance to get to the Final Four. Temple has a host of fine players—including 6'10" senior Lamont Barnes, 6'9" sophomore Kevin Lyde, 6'10" sophomore Ron Rollerson, 6'1" sophomore Lynn Greer, and Wadley—returning from last year's NCAA Tournament, where they lost to Duke.

"There's no telling how far we can go." Sanchez said. "We have a lot of experience on this team. We were one win away from the Final Four. Coach Chaney always does a good job of preparing for the tournament. He's had a lot of success here. We're going to work as hard as we can again to get back to the tournament. If we can do that, we should be all right."

Ex–Temple Star Prepares for a Shot at NBA Career

THE *PHILADELPHIA TRIBUNE*, AUGUST 3, 1999

When Lynard Stewart finished his basketball career with the Temple Owls, he was hoping to get an invitation to an NBA camp. However, Stewart, a 6'8", 210-pound forward, did have a chance to gain some professional experience before that. He and his brother Larry Stewart, a former Coppin State standout who spent some time with the Washington Bullets and the Seattle SuperSonics, played pro ball in Spain this season.

"I wanted to go to an NBA camp somewhere," Stewart said. "I just wanted a chance. You never know what can happen. I know Larry was invited to the Bullets as a free agent. The next thing you knew he had made the team.

"I had a great time in Spain. It was a good experience for me. They play some good basketball in Europe. The competition helps [me] prepare for the NBA. I'm not sure if I'll go back. I'm kind of waiting to see what happens this summer."

Stewart, a Simon Gratz product, has been playing summer basketball in the Baker League. Prior to playing in the Baker League, Stewart played in the Baltimore Coalition League.

"When Larry and I got back from Spain, we started playing in Baltimore," Stewart said. "The league had a lot of players from the city of Baltimore. We had a good time down there. Of course, everybody knows Larry because of his career at Coppin State. We saw Fang [Ron Mitchell, Coppin State head coach] all the time. My brother Stephen is finishing his education at Coppin State. Right now I'm playing in the Baker League and working out with John Hardnett during the day. I'm trying to stay ready in case an opportunity comes up."

Stewart, a four-year starter for the Owls, received several reports from his mother (Lois) on the Owls basketball team while he was in Spain. He was excited about the team's trip to the NCAA Elite Eight.

"I thought Temple did extremely well," said Stewart, who averaged 6.9 points and 5.2 rebounds a game in his senior year. "They went really far in the NCAA Tournament. I didn't get a chance to go to the regionals. We got killed by West Virginia [82–52] in the first round of the NCAA Tournament. I know they wanted to have a good showing after that game. That's one game I try to forget about.

"I'm glad my mother kept me informed throughout the season."

The Owls should be one of the top teams in the country this season. Some outstanding players, such as Lynn Greer, Mark Karcher, Lamont Barnes, Pepe Sanchez, and Kevin Lyde, are returning.

"They should have a real good team," Stewart said. "I've seen some of the players this summer. They seem to be ready for a big year. I haven't talked to coach [John] Chaney. I'm going to try to stop by his office soon."

In the meantime Stewart will be displaying his skills for pro scouts twice a week in the Baker League.

"I can't wait until next month," Stewart said. "There's going to be a lot of NBA players coming down. The games are only going to get better."

Ron Rollerson Ready
Whenever He's Needed

THE *PHILADELPHIA TRIBUNE*, JANUARY 11, 2000

When Ron Rollerson first attended one of John Hardnett's workouts at the Palestra two years ago, he played against former Temple star Marc Jackson, who is currently playing professional basketball in Europe. Rollerson saw how Jackson maneuvered around the basket for rebounds and put-backs. He noticed how easily he stepped outside for jump shots.

Rollerson, who was entering his freshman year at Temple, learned a great deal from playing against Jackson. The former south Jersey star from Faith Christian Academy has tried to provide the same kind of play for the Owls.

"I remember playing against a lot of people at John Hardnett's workouts," Rollerson said. "I had to play Theo Ratliff, Jason Lawson, and a lot of guys. But Marc Jackson really impressed me. He didn't do anything fancy on the court. He would just come down the lane and get good position. Marc would do everything smoothly. He played aggressively, too. I'm trying to be more aggressive on the court."

The Owls' 6'10", 290-pound sophomore leads the team with 51.7 percent shooting from the field. He grabbed a career-high nine rebounds against Villanova. He also scored nine points in 16 minutes in the Owls' Big 5 victory over the Wildcats. Rollerson has done a nice job of filling in for Kevin Lyde, who has been troubled with back spasms periodically throughout the season.

"I don't always get a lot of playing time," said Rollerson, who averages 2.2 points and 2.9 rebounds a game. "I play between eight and ten minutes a game. I just try to be productive when I'm out there.

"I want to be able to get some baskets and rebounds for us. I want to be a presence in the middle of the defense. We have a lot of guys who can score, like Lynn [Greer], Mark [Karcher], Quincy [Wadley], and Lamont [Barnes]. So there's not a lot of pressure on me."

Temple (with a 7–3 record overall, 1–0 league) recently dropped out of the Associated Press top 25. However, the Owls' point guard, Pepe Sanchez, has returned to the starting lineup after being sidelined since November 21 with a right ankle sprain.

"It's great to have Pepe back," Rollerson said. "He's an outstanding point guard. He handles the ball extremely well. He plays excellent defense. Plus, he brings a lot of leadership to our team. He's going to make a big difference."

The Owls are certainly going to need Sanchez, Karcher, Lyde, and everyone else healthy to make a strong run in the NCAA Tournament.

"We have to stay away from injuries," Rollerson said. "That's hard to do sometimes. But I think if we can remain healthy and play good basketball, there's no telling how far we can go this year."

Former Temple Star
Lands Coaching Job

THE *PHILADELPHIA TRIBUNE*, JULY 25, 2000

Jason Ivey didn't expect to get into the coaching profession. He had enjoyed a four-year career playing basketball for Temple that included four consecutive trips to the NCAA Tournament. He played in the CBA for a year. He even played some professional basketball in Australia and China.

Ivey returned to Temple to finish his education last season. He was fortunate enough to receive a graduate assistantship in the Owls' basketball office. Once again, coaching didn't cross his mind until Temple assistant coach Dean Demopoulos decided to accept the head coaching position at University of Missouri–Kansas City. Demopoulos asked Ivey to join his staff as an assistant, and Ivey couldn't turn him down.

"I was really excited," Ivey said. "I really appreciate all the things Dean has done for me as a player. But this was just a great opportunity for me. I was using the graduate assistantship to help me finish my coursework in my major, human resources. I used to answer the phones in the office. I would talk about basketball to coach [John] Chaney, Nate [Blackwell],

Dan [Leibovitz], and John DiSangro all the time. Of course, they were very knowledgeable."

Ivey will try to use that knowledge in his new position.

"I know Dean has everything broken down," Ivey said. "He's going to go over everything with me. I'm just getting my feet wet right now. It's possible I could work with the big men. I'll just have to wait and see."

Ivey, a 6'7" forward, played at Temple from 1993–96. In his freshman year he helped the Owls advance to the NCAA Elite Eight.

"That was a great season," Ivey said. "The only thing we wanted was to take coach Chaney [to] the Final Four. I played with Aaron [McKie], Eddie [Jones], and Rick [Brunson]. I was fortunate to play with some good players. All these guys are in the NBA. My job was just to rebound, play defense, and hit some open shots. Everybody knew about Eddie, Aaron, and Rick. They actually opened things up for me."

Missouri–Kansas City is a member of the Mid-Continent Conference. The team finished with an overall 16-13 record last season. Missouri–Kansas City has several returning players including Michael Jackson, the conference Player of the Year.

"We should have a pretty good year," Ivey said. "I'm looking forward to the season. I have to take a look at the schedule again. It's a pretty tough schedule. We don't have one as tough as Temple. But I think we play some pretty good teams."

Owls' Wadley
Happy to Be Back

THE *PHILADELPHIA TRIBUNE*, NOVEMBER 21, 2000

John Chaney knows more than anybody about the value of a great player. He's also an expert on the NCAA's academic policy and Proposition 48. That's why he was happy when Quincy Wadley was awarded an extra year of eligibility by the NCAA.

Wadley, the 6'4" guard, averaged 12.8 points and 3.9 assists a game last year. He was a huge part of the Owls' Atlantic 10 Conference championship team.

"Quincy is certainly a bright spot on our ballclub academically," Chaney said. "He was the first one in America, I would imagine, to gain his year back by completing the academic credits necessary to graduate within the specified time. Secondly, he's pretty special, because now with him coming back, it gives us a little bit more experience than was once expected. Quincy brings a tremendous ability to fight hard on the defensive end. He's also one of our leaders along with Lynn Greer and Kevin Lyde."

Wadley is excited about being with the Owls. He knew there was a possibility of coming back. However, the former Harrisburg High basketball star didn't know for sure until the NCAA contacted the school in the spring.

"It was good news," said Wadley, who earned his undergraduate degree in African-American studies last summer. "I really wanted to come back. I didn't like the way our season ended against Seton Hall (a 67–65 loss in the NCAA Tournament).

"Basically, I just worked extremely hard on and off the court. I tried not to think about the extra year too much. But I'm glad to be here. I see a lot of potential in this year's team."

The Owls got off to a slow start. So far, they've defeated Delaware and New Mexico in the preseason NIT. And on Friday night they ruined John Calipari's debut as Memphis coach by defeating the Tigers, 67–62.

"It's going to take awhile for everybody to jell," Wadley said. "Lynn, Kevin, and myself have the most experience. Although Ron [Rollerson] and Alex [Wesby] were here last year, we still have a lot of new faces like Carlton [Aaron], Ron Blackshear, and David Hawkins. We'll be all right."

No Rest for Aching Lyde
Until Owls Are Finished

THE *PHILADELPHIA TRIBUNE*, MARCH 23, 2001

There's no rest for the weary. Lynn Greer will continue to lead the country in minutes played. John Chaney, Temple head coach, can't afford to take Greer off the court. He needs his 6'1" junior on the court to run the offense.

He also needs Kevin Lyde, the Owls' 6'9", 260-pound center, on the floor. Like Greer, Lyde is playing a lot of minutes, but he's lumbering up and down the court with a sore left Achilles tendon. Neither Greer nor Lyde will be able to rest until after the season.

Lyde hasn't practiced with the team in the last three weeks. He only plays in games, and skips practice, because of his injury. In spite of the soreness, he played 63 minutes in the victories over Texas and Florida. He averaged 10.5 points and 4.5 rebounds a game. He has to lace up his sneakers again tonight at 10:00 P.M. as Temple faces Penn State in the NCAA South regional semifinal at the Georgia Dome in Atlanta.

"Kevin has given us so much," Chaney said. "Here's a guy who can't even practice. He can only play in the games. He just goes out and gives us a tremendous effort. Kevin is one of the best big men in the country. He's one of the best kids I've ever had."

Lyde plans to continue as Temple's inside presence around the basket. The former Oak Hill Academy star has developed a nice jump hook from about eight feet away from the basket. He can spot up and hit the jumper. On defense he's become a major threat with his shot-blocking skills.

He finished the regular season as the national leader in offensive rebounds with a total of 130 in 29 games, an average of 4.5 per game. He also finished the season ranked third in the Atlantic 10 Conference for overall rebounding (9.0 rpg) behind A-10 Player of the Year David West of Xavier (11.0 rpg) and Bill Phillips of St. Joseph's (9.3 rpg).

"When I'm on the court, I want to win," said Lyde, who has been battling tendinitis in his foot. "It's no pain, no gain. I'm not going to be able to relax until after the season. I give all I've got for as long as I can. So far it's been working all right. I haven't been tired. I give it 110 percent. It's a reaction to just wanting to be a basketball player. You want to go out there and give it your all."

Greer has been very impressed with Lyde's production on the court. He realizes his good friend and teammate has done everything he can to help the team despite the difficult circumstances.

"Kevin's played really well," Greer said. "He's got a sore foot. He doesn't complain about the discomfort. He just comes out and plays his game. I'm glad he's playing because we definitely need him. If we're going to get past Penn State, we have to get something from Kevin."

Lyde is one of five McDonald All-Americans to have played for Chaney. The others include Rick Brunson, Mark Macon, Mark Karcher, and Donald Hodge. Lyde averages 34.7 minutes a game. His two free throws with 14 seconds to play pulled the Owls within a point and paved the way for Greer's game-winning foul shots in the A-10 semifinal win over George Washington.

Temple Star Plays in China; Lynn Greer Shows Off His Skills

THE *PHILADELPHIA TRIBUNE*, AUGUST 24, 2001

I t's not every year that a Temple basketball player has the opportunity to play for one of the national touring teams. Aaron McKie and Eddie Jones were allowed to participate on some of the All-Star teams with USA Basketball and, five years ago, former Owl Lynard Stewart played for one of the teams.

Now Lynn Greer, Temple's brilliant guard, is among the 12 top players who have been chosen to represent their country in the World University Games.

"I'm a little tired right now," said Greer, who called from Beijing, China. "I'm still getting used to the time difference. It's a 12-hour difference from here to Philly. It's around 86 degrees. There's no humidity like in Philly.

"This is a great opportunity for me. I get a chance to represent my country. I appreciate coach [John] Chaney letting me come over here. I remember going into his office and telling him about it. I explained to him that I wanted to play in the World University Games. He told me it was all right. After that, I was really excited. I knew I had a chance to play against some good competition."

The World University Games, held every two years, is a multisport competition open to athletes between the ages of 17 and 28 (born between January 1, 1973, and December 31, 1983) who are or have been students at a college or university within the past year. This summer the games will be held in Beijing. The men's basketball competition, currently featuring teams from 27 countries, has been divided into eight preliminary-round pools. Placed into Pool B, the United States will face Turkey tonight. Quarterfinals are scheduled to be played August 26–28 with the semifinals slated for August 30. The gold medal will be contested on August 31. With a 40-game winning streak at the Games and having captured six consecutive gold medals, the USA has been a dominating force at the Games since the competition was created in 1965. The United States has earned an incredible 16 medals in as many appearances at the Games, including twelve golds, three silvers, and one bronze, and holds an amazing 110–6 (.984 winning percentage) record.

"I want to win a gold medal," Greer said. "We have a lot of good players like Juan Dixon [Maryland] and Chris Owens [Texas]. We've been playing very well together. Jerry Dunn [Penn State head coach] is our coach.

"When we're not practicing, we usually talk about last season. For example, we played against Maryland two years ago. So, Juan and I have talked about the game. We played against Chris in the NCAA Tournament. Of course, we played against Penn State in the NCAA Tournament too."

Greer's father, Lynn Sr., uncle, and cousin have made the long trip to China to watch him play. His mother, Alma, and sister, Kelli, stayed home.

"I'm going to bring something back for them," Greer said. "I don't know what I'm going to bring back. But I know it has to be more than just a T-shirt. I'm going to try to look around for something really nice. You don't come to China every day."

It's been a busy summer for Greer. He spent a lot of time working out with John Hardnett and Fred Douglas, two of the city's outstanding basketball clinicians.

"The workouts really prepared me for this level," Greer said.

Milt Colston Recalls
His Old Coach;
John Chaney Honored at
Hall of Fame This Weekend

THE *PHILADELPHIA TRIBUNE*, OCTOBER 5, 2001

Milt Colston has told a lot of people about playing for John Chaney during his coaching career at Cheyney State. He is excited about Chaney being inducted into the Basketball Hall of Fame—and you can't blame him.

Colston played a major part in Chaney's success. In 1978 he and his teammates—Gilbert Saunders, Gerald Mills, Arthur Stone, Jeffery Hutchinson, Roger Leysath, Andrew Fields, Kenny Hynson, and Charles Murphy—led the Wolves to an NCAA Championship.

"When I heard about coach Chaney going into the Hall of Fame, I thought about the national championship team right away," he said. "I know that was a big part of his career. It was special for me too. He had a lot to do with our success. It's good to see him get the recognition he deserves."

Colston, an All–Public League standout at Olney High, was a Division II All-American at Cheyney State. He was known for his deadly jump shot and his ability to get his shot off at any time. He was a clutch player in many big games.

"Coach Chaney had a lot of confidence in me," said Colston, who scored over 1,000 points during his college career. "I never worried about missing shots. He really allowed me to play my game. I don't think he's changed a lot since his days at Cheyney. I think our teams ran a little bit more than his Temple teams. Other than that, coach Chaney doesn't like turnovers and wants his teams to play good defense. He knows how to get the most out of his players."

Colston, 44, is the assistant director of student activities at Cheyney. He and his wife, Maxine, have a two-year-old daughter, Laurin. Colston stays in contact with Chaney on a regular basis.

"We usually get together and play tennis in the summer," Colston said. "He's a pretty good tennis player. He likes to play doubles. He knows how to slice the ball over the net. The good thing about coach Chaney is that he always brings food with him. We usually play at Awbury Recreation Center. He brings crabs, fruit, and vegetables. He likes sweet potatoes and okra. After we finish playing tennis, we sit around and talk about the good times."

Chaney was noted for recruiting a lot of top Public League players at Cheyney State. Some of his best players were from the city.

"Every year he would go to the Sonny Hill League and bring some players to Cheyney," Colston said. "He would provide guys like myself, Dana Clark, and Gil Saunders with a chance to play some good basketball. We had plenty of fun. We got a nice education. You can't ask for more than that."

John Chaney's Hall of Fame Speech

THIS PRESENTATION IS REPRINTED HERE
WITH THE PERMISSION OF THE *OWL SCOOP*, OCTOBER 13, 2001

Introductory Video Narrated by Emcee Ahmad Rashad

With over 650 victories in 29 seasons, John Chaney is one of the winningest coaches in college basketball history. He is a man who is never shy about showing his emotions, but he's also inspired strong emotions among others, earning the admiration of fans and players alike.

With his emphasis on discipline and hard work, Chaney commands respect among his players. And the workday starts early, as John is famous for his 5:00 A.M. practice sessions. Under the guidance of Chaney, the Owls have won 20 or more games in 15 seasons. His teams are known for their intensity, but none of his players are more intense than their coach.

Coach Chaney has built a winning tradition at Temple, but his legacy isn't just about basketball. It's also the many lives he's touched along the way.

Video Message from Bill Cosby

Well, John, I guess you're in. Somebody knew about your background, one that was very, very down and depressed, and against all odds—and that background, very few people know, was created by you. [Laughter.]

You could have done better for yourself. But you're just that kind of person that nobody liked. [Laughter.] That's why you were there. Not many parents move out and don't tell the child. [Laughter.]

So anyway, it seems that they believe you've risen above all of that. So congratulations. I guess you'll get some sort of trophy or something. [Laughter.] They called me and they asked me to chip in, and I just couldn't do it, John, I'm sorry. [Laughter and applause.]

Presentation by Hall of Fame Coach John Thompson

The last time I was at this podium, I cried. [Applause.] The next time I cried was when I heard that John Chaney was voted into the Hall of Fame. [Laughter.] And it was for a different reason.

I haven't been able to participate as much in a lot of events recently because I haven't felt well. As we were driving up last night, and I was really feeling bad, my nephew turned around and looked at me and asked me, "Do you want to turn around and go home, unc?" I said, "No." And he said, "Damn, you must love this man." I said, "Shut up, boy, and keep driving."

I can't say enough about John; the things that I respect him for are the things that you don't always see in the coaching fraternity.

One thing that I respect him for is the fact that he's a great coach. That goes without saying, and I guess that's the reason why a lot of folks think he's here.

The second reason why I have a great deal of respect for him is the fact that he's a tremendous teacher. Often when guys prepare students for the world that they have to live in today, it's misunderstood by so many people. But John has done a tremendous job directing young men in the right direction.

The third thing, which is probably one of the most significant things to me, is that while he was doing a very difficult job, he didn't neglect his obligation to address the social issues that pertained to so many kids who were *not* under his care. And that's an enormous distraction if you have only selfish goals.

When he called me and asked me to present him, I was extremely flattered. I'm speechless, and that's not one of my characteristics. But I want to say that that's a man's man, a coach's coach, a player's teacher. You've just got a special individual here. And I would not have come if I didn't love you, my brother. And I say that sincerely. For what you did, I love you.

Another thing I'm going to tell you: coming up here, my nephew also asked me, "Aren't you nervous about being in a crowd because of what's going on now?" [This event took place soon after September 11, 2001.] I said, "Well, you've got Mike Krzyzewski being inducted into the Hall of Fame." I think that if he weren't a coach and he stayed in the military, he would be one of those special service guys. Mike is really smart. Mike is the kind of guy that is a lot more militant than a lot of you think. And then you walk in the Hall of Fame, and you've got Bobby Knight *and* John Chaney. Now what terrorist is going to come in here and mess with them? This has got to be the safest place in America with those two guys here. And I say that respectfully, because I have an awful lot of respect for both of those men.

I also want to commend Mo [Malone] for being there. Mo, I could have said "Fo, Fo, Fo" too if you had come to Georgetown.

But without going on any further, I just can't think of any more words to say about him [Chaney]. I present to you John Chaney. [Fifty-two seconds of applause.]

Induction by Hall of Fame Board of Trustees Chairman Dave Gavitt

John Chaney, your career has been one remarkable success after another. You may call yourself old-fashioned; we call you simply one of the greatest teacher/coaches there has ever been in this game. You have been a mentor for so many, you have inspired so many, and you are completely respected by your colleagues across the country.

For all of these achievements—and for being such a special person to this game—by vote of the honors committee, by the power vested in the board of trustees, it is my privilege to induct you as a coach into the Naismith Memorial Basketball Hall of Fame, with all rights and privileges. [Twenty-three seconds of applause.]

Acceptance Speech by Coach John Chaney

I'm filled with a lot of humility. I think my emotions for the last couple days have just been on a roller coaster.

I can't help but feel somewhat apologetic; I've been really embarrassed about something, and I want to apologize to the committee. A few years back, we were asked to make contributions to the new building. And I pledged some money, certainly not as much as Mike [Krzyzewski]—you don't make that kind of money coming from Temple. But I pledged a significant amount of money, and paid it out over a couple years.

So one morning I was coming out of the shower at about 10:00 in the morning, and the phone rang and I picked the phone up, and somebody said, "Coach, this is the Hall of Fame," and I said, "I don't give a damn who you are, you're not getting any more money."

So I want to apologize. But after getting this ring, I certainly will be making some more donations.

When I talk about humility, I remember coming out of my house and getting into my car. I have a very small house—I'm in a row home. I've been there all my life. Although my wife would like us to get out, my neighbors would not like to see me leave. Anyway, a bus had been rerouted because they had some kind of construction work going on, and the bus came down my street, filled with people. I ran out of my house to get in my car, and the bus stopped, and the bus driver got off the bus and said to me, "Aren't you John Chaney?" I said, "Yes." And he said, "I thought you'd be living in a mansion."

But the people on the bus said, "Damn John Chaney. We're going to be late for work. Get your ass back in the bus!" Now if that doesn't tell you what kind of person you are, then nothing will. I'm talking about humility.

Now, I have a satellite on top of my house, bigger than my house. My wife likes to look at soap operas from all over the world, and I want to see basketball games. When we got it, my son and I went up with the workers, climbed up on the roof, and we were working to put the satellite up. We got it all up, and once it was done, everybody went down, and they had to call the fire department to get my ass down.

Humility. You just work all your life, but you never, ever think about accolades, or think about receiving awards or anything else.

You see, I came from a situation where the counselors decided what curriculum you would go into. They decided if you would go into college preparatory or industrial arts—you know, machine shop, wood shop. Well, they made the choice for me, and I was very uncomfortable; beating my fingers with the hammer in the wood shop wasn't good. Making cookie cutters was something that I didn't like doing.

My stepfather was a carpenter. I don't know who my real father was. But my stepfather was a carpenter, and I tried to find a way to get out of that—so I would make bad cookie cutters, and they took me out of the machine shop. I had to beg.

And then when they put me in the wood shop, I found myself making stools, four-legged stools. I found the stool was a little uneven, so I cut a leg off, and suddenly the stool would lean to this side. So I cut another leg off, and I kept cutting legs off until I had a tabletop.

They took me out of there and put me in college preparatory, where I really wanted to be. But I was no different than a lot of the other youngsters. I just wanted to play in the sandbox. I wanted to dribble a basketball all my life. I had no aspirations to go to college at that time. My mother worked very hard, and sent us to high school, and we figured that if we got out of high school, that was it. You go to high school and then you go out and get a nine-to-five job, because at that time that was the mentality.

Of all the schools in the city, I think Temple had maybe one black player at the time. But there were no dormitories. Youngsters were getting partial scholarships. People don't even know what that is today. Partial scholarships meant that you received tuition and you had to commute.

Well, they couldn't afford for me to go back and forth to college. They were just happy that I had graduated from high school. But I was very fortunate; I had a great high school coach, a Jewish man by the name of Sam Browne, who passed away a couple years ago, who would not allow me to do anything but go on to college. And he worked extremely hard trying to convince my parents that I should go to college.

In the summer he would buy us kids some clothes and take us out to the Poconos, to the mountains, where we'd be free from the gangs and all the problems in the city area.

He convinced my parents that I had an opportunity to go to school. That opportunity came one day when Big House Gaines came looking for me. I found myself at Bethune-Cookman College, one of the first land grant colleges in America; a black woman founded that school.

A lot of the black schools were sister schools. A lot of people don't understand that. They were sister schools. I believed so strongly in the black schools at that time, because they never, ever put a ceiling on what you could learn. They believed so strongly in building up the floor so you could reach all ceilings. They never said that there's a score that says you can't do it. And I believe strongly in that. They believed in access and opportunity, and they gave me that chance. And I think that it made a big difference in my life.

When I left there and came home, I eventually ended up at Gratz High School, where I met one of our great coaches— who is here tonight—William Ellerbee.

When I left there I went to Cheyney State. And of course the president there always said to me, "You'd be a Phi Beta if you could just learn how to spell your name."

Cheyney State was another land grant college. They believed so strongly in giving access and opportunity to youngsters— something that John [Thompson] and so many of us fought for

for so many years, to make sure people understand that youngsters should be given more opportunity, not less.

It was during my 10 years with the wonderful young people there that I learned how to cook. I learned how to cook things that I shouldn't cook. I remember we had a situation during the holidays where school was closed down, but we had games to play. So I would go over and steal the dishes from the lunchroom, steal long rows of eggs, and get boxes of grits, because you could take a box of grits and you could feed everybody in this room. And I would bring it over and I'd cook. Because I couldn't get a frying pan and the other things I needed to cook with, I went to the store and I got an aluminum pan. And I began to cook before the practice sessions, because we had to have breakfast. Well, I learned never to use aluminum pans when cooking eggs. The guys were running out of the building because the eggs were green. I couldn't convince them that they could eat their eggs, that it was all right. I even tried a little bit myself, and they would not believe that. So I learned what not to cook. I had to do that at that school for a long time.

Then finally I got a chance to meet somebody like Peter Liacouras, the first president I worked with at Temple. He spent some time with me and convinced me that I could come to Temple, and there was more that we could do.

Temple is a school that offers opportunity and access with its law school, its dental school, its hospital, all of the offerings in the inner city. And it will stay its course and not leave the inner city, but instead stay there and serve people who need. That convinced me to come to Temple, and I've never thought about leaving Temple, ever, ever.

Now I'm going to be a little lengthy, so Peter [Liacouras], you said that you might think about falling out. I'm going to be a little lengthy, because it is a special night in terms of thanking people. You just don't get here without thanking people. You bring these people in here and you must thank them. There's no way you could stand here and be brief—I don't think so. So you'll have to endure.

I want to introduce my family. My wife is here, and I'll tell her that there are diamonds in this [points to Hall of Fame ring], so I know you'll take this. My wife, Jeanne, is here. [The rest of his family introductions—daughter, Pamela, son John, son Darryl (who was not present), and four grandchildren—were drowned out by applause.] I'm very proud of all of them, and I can't help but believe that my wife has taken a lot from me, and I want to say to you that I appreciate you tolerating me all these years. But maybe I should quit now that I've got this.

I want to introduce the folks from my coaching staff who are also here: there's my first recruit at Temple, coach Nate Blackwell; coach Leibovitz; and, of course, my business manager, John DiSangro.

And certainly I can't miss out expressing how much I appreciate my secretary, who ran around all day because my family had to come by train, and the train was 40 minutes late, and they were only in here about 20 minutes or so before we could get over here. My secretary, Essie Davis, is here. I always say, when somebody's calling me that I don't like to hear from, I always say, "Tell him I'm not here." And she crosses herself before she does it, knowing that she's going to have to lie for me.

I want to give a special thanks to [Temple's] new president, President Adamany, and of course, the man who was with me all those years, President Peter Liacouras. He was always with me win or tie, and here he is here. Former Vice President James White is also here. He follows us just about everywhere we go.

And then my dear friend, my special friend Sonny Hill, who uses the word *I* all the time, is here. That word reminds me who's on the radio: it's a solid two hours of *I, I, I, I, I, I, I, I*. At least Al McGuire used to say the most important word in the English language is just two letters: *no*. Sonny uses *I* all the time. I'm very proud he could be here.

And then there's my friend Dr. Anthony Pinnie, who is a very close friend. He and I went to junior high school together. My mom used to make only two sandwiches. One was something she called mayonnaise, lettuce, and tomato. And then she made dessert: peanut butter and not jelly, but jam. So I had two sandwiches. And when I'd go to Barrett schoolyard for lunch, Tony Pinnie came in with an Italian sandwich. For the first time in my life I saw a sandwich that had broccoli rabe in it. I could not believe it. It was green. I had never eaten a green sandwich in my life. Tony is here today.

Speedy Morris is here, really one of my great friends and a brother to me in so many ways, with his wife, Mimi. Here's a story about him: when he coached La Salle, he was coaching with such fire and such effort and such energy that one day he split his pants. This is one for the comic strips. He split his pants right down the middle, and never stopped coaching. His wife saw this and got up and walked right behind him, with his coat hanging behind him, all the way to the dressing room, with needle and thread. While he was giving his team hell, she sewed him right up and he went right back out and never missed a minute. Now that's my kind of coach.

I'd also like to thank our trustees so much. I know that there are some here. Trustees are so solid in so many of our universities. They change so many different things involved in sports. They make life better for the students, without question, with their support. Not only just their ideas and legislation, but with their support from the standpoint of money. In building our new facility, I know that our trustees gave up a lot of money—much more than Billy [Cosby] did. Billy didn't give a dime. We begged Billy for lots of money and he didn't give us anything. He just wanted to speak.

So I want to make sure that I recognize them [the trustees]: Mr. Howard Gittis, Lew Katz, Mr. Leibovitz, and so many others who are here tonight. My thanks to Joan Ballots, who follows our team just about everywhere. You've got to stay out of the lobby, Joan. I'm getting a little tired of you waiting for us.

There are some mentors here that I would like to make mention of.

We already know about John [Thompson]. Thank God that John is here, because he could have been on one of those flights from that perverted situation that happened [September 11]. I love him to death. He's someone that so many of us admire. He's one of my mentors.

And I've never, ever forgotten him calling me on the day that he was walking out [of a game to protest Proposition 48]. And Peter can probably remember telling me, "Whatever you want to do—if you want to walk out, you just do that." John, I'm very proud of you and I love you. You often bring tears to my eyes when I look at you because I love you so much.

I also need to thank John McLendon, who passed away—a mentor, great innovator, great coach.

Ray Meyer is here.

Al McGuire, who passed away, used to write me letters saying, "Stop scheduling those tough teams. Stay away from Duke." I didn't listen to him.

I know why you're in the Hall of Fame, Mike [Krzyzewski]—because you've been beating my butt all these years.

Vivian Stringer is here somewhere. Vivian and I used to open up the sashes and boys and girls would practice together— something that was unheard of.

I called Vivian's mother and talked to her, and we talked about Vivian's husband, who passed away. And we talked about so many times when she showed so much strength and so much character with all of the tragedies that happened in her family. Her father passed away when we were at Cheyney together. And her daughter was stricken with spinal meningitis. I hope that she's doing well now. But certainly she's had to bear these problems all these years. And then this past summer her young son was in an automobile accident and now he's doing fine. In fact, he attends my camp, and tries to run it all the time. She's gone through a lot.

She would call me, and my wife would say, "Who in the world are you talking with? You have to practice at 5:00, and you've been on the phone for two hours talking to coach Stringer."

Meanwhile Vivan's asking me about Xs and Os and she's got a speech somewhere, and what should be the theme. I said, "Vivian, the theme is going to be me doing something with you if you don't get off this phone. I've got to go to practice in two hours." But I later learned that she's been practicing in the morning, too, so I'm happy to see you here.

One of my mentors, Nolan Richardson, is not here. But he is one of my mentors.

Tom Gola is here—a guy that was a great All-American at a time when Philly really was very exciting. He brought Speedy in here, and Speedy, I don't know if he paid for your ticket or not. He had the nerve to give that little guy, what's his name, Robin Deutsch [Hall of Fame staff member]—he had the nerve to give him a watch, and told him when he left here that it was a Rolex, and it was a Rotech.

Lou Carnesecca could not be here. He called me to say he's been having to go to a lot of funerals because of the tragedy that happened in New York. And he could not be here.

And then there's Harry Litwack, who was one of our great Hall of Famers. Harry was someone that I would go and watch all the time, and watch his old 3-2 zone, and of course you know that [Jack] Ramsey was here, who coached at St. Joe years ago. We watched these guys and marveled at what they did. You could always steal a few ideas and add them to your own. Harry was someone that I really admired so much.

And then there's a young man that had contracted polio; he contracted polio one year before they found a vaccine for it. His name was Victor Harris. I gained so much from him because when we would play, like Tommy [Gola], we'd all play out in a league called the Narberth League, where they had some of the great players. Sonny [Hill] and all of us played out there. [Harris] would find a way to come and get me, because he knew that I didn't have carfare. But yet he was in a wheelchair. That to me was something very special. And I never will forget it.

I'd like to recognize some of my coaches who've left if they're here. Coach Dean Demopoulos, who is now working in Seattle, and telling them lies about how to play my zone. You didn't learn enough. And of course Jay Norman, he is someone that worked with us, and he also played at Temple and is one of Temple's greats. And I wanted to bring recognition to him.

I honestly feel that when I look at my life, I look at it in stages, where I think that it's nothing but faces and memories. Great faces, great memories. One was a coach by the name of Jim Maloney who worked with me for many years. John

[Thompson], Jim even called you about his daughter. He was a God-fearing man. He had five youngsters, and he named them all after books of the Bible. And I think you helped the only girl get into Georgetown, and she's graduating this year. You didn't give her any money, John, I know you.

I can remember this with Jimmy: Jimmy knew that I agonized whenever I'd lose a game. And I'd go through stretches where if I'd lose two or three games, then I'd come into the office beating up on myself. I was hard on myself for making mistakes. Sometimes I would take it out on the players, too, but most of the time it was always me. This one morning I got in really early, and Jimmy was right around me because our areas were very close. And Jimmy was a guy that went to church every day. And as I walked in I started cussing and fussing and saying what a cruel world this is. Everyone's against me. I hate everybody, and I'm going to kill 'em when they get here to practice. This was just before practice. I said, "I think the Lord even hates me."

And Jimmy jumped straight up, and he walked right around and did like this [puts his finger to his mouth].

And he said, "Coach," and I said, "What the hell do you want?" He said, "Shhh . . . you've got to remember, Coach, the Lord always comes, but sometimes He's late." I said, "Get out of this office."

He was a guy who would get Al McGuire and so many of the coaches to come in and sit down and chew the fat. I miss him. I miss him very, very much.

If I have any players here that have made any contribution at all, I'd like them to stand up. The effect that you've had on my life has been something very special. I don't wish to call out your names, because I think that I might miss somebody.

I want you to know I have already had something made to go into a case where they put memorabilia here. And I sent them some things already. This picture I had made epitomizes just about everything that I stand for. It speaks so highly of so many of the youngsters that I've had in my program, especially the ones that have come from one-parent families, or even no-parent families. There's a growing number of those among youngsters who play basketball. This is a little picture that I have up on my wall of a youngster, an athlete, a young person who is just laying in the bed on a mattress with absolutely no sheet on the bed, holes in the wall. Perhaps you could imagine that all kinds of vermin might be in that room where he's sleeping. And on the bed there's a football.

At the top of the picture it says, "Dreamers." And I want to read to you what else it says, which came from a Scottish poet by the name of William Yeats. It says here, "I, being poor, have only my dreams; I spread my dreams under your feet; tread softly, because you just might tread on my dreams."

I say with all sincerity that we have youngsters growing up whose dreams, believe me, only come up to some of our feet. And you must recognize that whether you're teaching youngsters or whether you're working—I don't care what you're in— you ought to recognize that young people have simple dreams. And these dreams don't materialize in many of our inner cities.

I'd appreciate this being put in my case, because this is what many of us stand for. Thank you so much.

Big Five Grads Prepare
for New Season Overseas

THE *PHILADELPHIA TRIBUNE*, JUNE 14, 2002

L evan Alston was getting loose—doing his stretching exercises with athletic trainer Keith Hall at La Salle's Tom Gola Arena. While Alston, a former Simon Gratz and Temple basketball star, was working out, Allen Iverson and Philadelphia 76ers guard Aaron McKie were playing four-on-four. And Marc Jackson, a Temple product who now plays for the Minnesota Timberwolves, was practicing his post-up moves.

It's that time of year for professional basketball players. With the NBA Draft coming up on June 26, the veterans want to stay in shape and the young players—like Na'im Crenshaw (St. Joseph's), Malik Moore (American International College), and Rasual Butler (La Salle)—work out to keep their skills sharp.

But for guys like Alston, it's time to get ready for another season of professional basketball abroad. Alston, a 6'2" guard, has played five seasons in China. The ex–Public League standout plans to go back in a few months.

"It's been great playing in China," Alston said. "I had a chance to play against Yao Ming. He's a pretty good player.

He can play in the NBA. He's 7'5". He can shoot and handle the ball. I know the Houston Rockets are thinking about taking him in the draft. I'm really fortunate to be playing basketball as a professional. I've played against a lot of American and Chinese players over the years. Basketball has expanded worldwide. It's big in China and getting bigger."

Alston is one of many local players playing pro basketball abroad. The list includes Michael Jordan (Penn, Venezuela), Jerome Allen (Penn, Italy), Geoff Owens (Penn, Poland), Lamont Barnes (Temple, Italy), Rasheed Brokenborough (Temple, Austria), Lynard Stewart (Temple, England), Mark Karcher (Temple, France), Pepe Sanchez (Temple, Greece), Donnie Carr (La Salle, Turkey), Paul Burke (La Salle, Italy), Michael Brooks (La Salle, France), K'Zell Wesson (La Salle, Italy), Andre Howard (St. Joseph's, Spain), Rashid Bey (St. Joseph's, Poland), Wil Johnson (St. Joseph's, England), Terrell Myers (St. Joseph's, England), Rob Haskins (St. Joseph's, Israel), Frank Wilkins (St. Joseph's, Mexico), and Dmitri Domani (St. Joseph's, Russia).

"It's a great opportunity for a lot of former college players," said James Henderson, an Orlando, Florida, based sports agent. "Some guys spend a year or two overseas. Then they come back and give the NBA another turn. If that doesn't work out, they can usually go back. Plus, they can make good money in Europe."

The best players in Europe make between $1 and $2 million a year. The average players in the top division earn between $150,000 and $200,000 a year. The second- and third-level players pull down between $30,000 and $40,000 a season. The players also receive housing and living expenses.

Justin Zanik, a sports agent with the Mark Bartelstein agency in Chicago, Illinois, has placed more than 20 players abroad. Zanik knows the well-paying markets overseas.

"If you have some NBA experience, it's a lot easier to get a big contract," Zanik said. "There aren't a lot of guys making over a million dollars playing in Europe. However a guy playing six months in Italy, Spain, or Greece can earn somewhere near $165,000 a season. They're the top-level teams. The second tier would be France, Turkey, and Israel. The next level down would be Germany and Belgium. The big thing for the players is learning the language and adjusting to the lifestyle."

Roland Houston, La Salle University's assistant basketball coach, played 12 years of professional basketball abroad. Houston played in Nice, LeMans, and Limonges, all in France, then on to Spain, Argentina, and Israel before coming back to Philadelphia.

"I played against a lot of guys from Philly like Michael Brooks, Richie Laurel, Victor Alexander, and Terence Stansbury," said Houston, who played basketball for Martin Luther King High and Rhode Island. "The games are very competitive. They usually only have one or two Americans on each team. There is some pressure to win. The countries don't like to lose. Fortunately, I had a successful career in Europe. I took advantage of all the cultural activities, customs, language, and the food. It was a great experience for me."

Note: For more information on pro basketball in Europe, contact www.eurobasket.com.

Gratz Varsity Taps New Coach

THE *PHILADELPHIA TRIBUNE*, OCTOBER 4, 2002

Leonard Poole, who always wanted to be head basketball coach at Simon Gratz High School, has seen his dream become a reality.

Poole will take over for Bill Ellerbee, who coached the Bulldogs for 20 years, winning six Public League championships and compiling a 451–100 record. Last summer Ellerbee retired as a teacher and later joined Temple head coach John Chaney's basketball staff as an assistant.

"It's certainly a dream come true," Poole said. "I'm looking forward to coaching the team. You can't replace coach Ell. He had size 98 shoes. I think mine are size 12s. What we're going to do is keep the program moving. We're going to maintain our level of excellence. And we have the players who can get it done for us. This means a lot to the school and to me."

There's no question about that. Poole, a 1971 Simon Gratz alumnus, dearly loves his school. He was a terrific basketball player for the Bulldogs.

Poole played for Chaney during his coaching days at Gratz. He played with some great players, such as Joe Anderson, Leon

White, and Al Walker. After his playing days at Gratz he was an All–Pennsylvania State Athletic Conference backcourt ace for East Stroudsburg University. He also played in the Continental Basketball Association for the Wilkes-Barre Barons and in the Charles Baker League.

Poole is currently the school's head football coach. He has been the Bulldogs' junior varsity coach for the last four years. In addition to working with Ellerbee, he has learned a great deal about the game from Chaney and others.

Poole's knowledge and experience in basketball is built around hard work and discipline.

"I played for coach Chaney, who is a real taskmaster," Poole said. "All the guys I grew up playing basketball for—Sonny Hill and Vince Miller—they were taskmasters too. Coach Ell had everybody working hard. We're not going to change. I don't know any other way to get things done. Hard work breeds success."

Tyree Watson, Simon Gratz's brilliant shooting guard, believes Poole will do a fine job.

"I know coach Ell's departure is a huge loss," Watson said, "but I played for Mr. Poole on his JV team. He has all the qualities necessary to be a great head coach on varsity. Everything is going to be fine with Mr. Poole. I can't wait for the season to get started."

Wesby's Work Habits
Win Chaney's Praise

THE *PHILADELPHIA TRIBUNE*, NOVEMBER 1, 2002

When Alex Wesby goes back to his North Philadelphia neighborhood, near 28th and Cecil B. Moore, he walks proudly throughout his community. And Wesby, Temple's 6'6" basketball star, *should* feel good about his success on and off the court.

Many people know about Wesby's basketball exploits. In 1998 he led Ben Franklin High to the Public League championship. He averaged 19.3 points and 13 rebounds a game. He was the city's top player.

Wesby came to Temple the following year. He was able to practice with the Owls but, under the NCAA guidelines, did not play. He has gone on to play three seasons for the Owls. Now he has his final year of eligibility and will be in a cherry and white uniform when Temple opens its season against Rutgers at Liacouras Center on November 24.

He was able to earn the extra year because of his hard work in the classroom. Last summer Wesby graduated from Temple with his degree in tourism, hospitality, and management.

"I had to take a class called 'Intro to Management,'" Wesby said. "After that, I had to do a senior project. I did an internship with Advantage Unlimited in west Philly. It's a special events company. I was involved with doing media and community relations. I wrote press releases and put together databases for different events.

"I helped to promote the Mayor's Walk. It was very successful. A lot of people came to the event. The walk started at Eakins Oval and went down to Penn's Landing. I didn't get a chance to meet Mayor [John] Street. But I did meet Bernard Hopkins [middleweight champion] that day.

"I actually graduated in August. The ceremony was in September at Mitten Hall. I graduated with Derrick Battie [former Temple star]. His brother, Tony Battie, who plays for the Boston Celtics, was there. We had coach [John] Chaney, Nate [Blackwell, assistant coach], Dan [Leibovitz, assistant coach], and Mr. [Bill] Ellerbee [assistant coach] at the ceremony. Eddie Hurtt was there too."

Chaney is very impressed with Wesby's work ethic and determination. He has never been a fan of the NCAA's rigid academic requirements, going all the way back to Proposition 48 in the eighties. However Chaney was pleased with Wesby's efforts to complete his academic requirements to be eligible for this season.

"He had to fight like the dickens for 500 hours to get his degree by the end of August," Chaney said. "He accomplished that. He gets his year back. Losing that year was a punishment from the NCAA for being a Prop 48. I think he's about the sixth person who has gotten his degree as a Prop 48. I think we lead the country in that. Everybody says you can't do it, it can't be done, when all you have to do is give kids access and opportunity.

"Alex is just like a son as far as I'm concerned. I've never had a kid like him. He does not miss a class. He's done everything we've asked him to do."

The ex–Public League standout didn't have it easy last season. He struggled through some rough times with the passing of his mother, Ella Mae Wesby. He missed one game due to that loss. He then missed five subsequent games in January due to a right wrist injury. Upon his return, the Owls were 12–3 down the stretch.

"Alex has always been a player who shows who he is with his deeds, because he is not someone who vocalizes," Chaney said. "He leads more by example and his play on the floor speaks louder than his words."

Wesby, a quiet leader, averaged 11.3 points and 5.9 rebounds a game this season. He needs 232 points to reach 1,000 career points and 110 rebounds to reach 500 in his career.

The Owls will miss three key starters in big men Kevin Lyde and Ron Rollerson and high-scoring guard Lynn Greer. But Wesby feels Temple will be able to compete in the Atlantic 10 Conference despite the loss of those three great players.

"It's going to be tough," said Wesby, who is cocaptain with backcourt ace David Hawkins. "Basically, we lost three starters. Lynn was a terrific player. He made a lot of big shots for us. Kevin and Ron were good players around the basket.

"We do have some good players coming back, like David Hawkins and Nile Murry. We have some great young players, like Maurice Collins [former Simon Gratz standout], Antywane Robinson, and Keith Butler.

"I would like to get back to the NCAA Tournament. Two years ago we went to the Final Eight. I think going to the NIT was a good experience for us. But we've got a lot of work to do in order to make the NCAA Tournament. Coach plays a tough schedule. So we're going to be tested right away."

If Wesby has a good season, he could get some NBA looks. He plays great defense. He rebounds the ball well for his size. He's a much-underrated ball-handler and shooter. But Wesby isn't banking on a pro basketball career.

"I wouldn't mind playing in the pros," Wesby said. "Obviously, that would be great. But I have my degree. I'm taking four classes now in sports management. I want to inspire others to do well.

"Coach Chaney has been a father figure to me. Eddie and John Hardnett have helped me too. I'm very fortunate to be where I am today."

League Trains NBA Hopefuls

THE *PHILADELPHIA TRIBUNE*, JANUARY 28, 2003

There are a host of players who want to play in the NBA every year. Unfortunately most of them go undrafted and some don't even get invited to NBA rookie and free-agent camps. For many years these players would perhaps play in the Continental Basketball Association (CBA), the International Basketball Association (IBL), or for some small country overseas.

Now these players can prepare for a possible NBA career by sharpening their skills in the National Basketball Development League. For Kevin Lyde, Ron Rollerson, Nate Johnson, and Jeff Myers, the NBDL could be their ticket to the NBA.

Lyde, a former Temple standout, finished his college career with more than 1,000 points and 1,000 rebounds. He averaged 8.6 points, 7.8 rebounds, and 1.4 blocks a game while leading the Owls to the NIT. Lyde was hoping some team would take him in the NBA Draft last summer, but that didn't happen. He also wanted to play professional basketball in Turkey. That didn't work out either. Needless to say, he's pleased to be playing for the NBDL's Greenville Groove, located in Greenville, South Carolina.

"I'm happy to be here," Lyde said. "It's a good place for me. I'm working on my game all the time. I'm in good shape. We have a lot of great players in the NBDL."

The 6'10", 260-pound power forward is averaging 8.7 points and 6.5 rebounds a game. Lyde knows this is a time when the NBA signs a lot of players to 10-day contracts so, although his numbers are pretty good, he tries not to think about being called up.

"If it happens, that would be great," Lyde said. "It's just that I can't be too concerned and lose my focus. I don't want anything to affect the way I'm playing right now."

The Groove, with a current record of 14–14, won the inaugural league championship last year. Greenville was led by former South Philadelphia High and Drexel star Jeff Myers, who received Defensive Player of the Year honors last year.

Myers worked out with local basketball clinicians John Hardnett and Fred Douglas last summer. He started the preseason with the Toronto Raptors, but suffered a cartilage tear in his right knee during training camp. The 6'2", 185-pound guard spent the next two months rehabbing his knee prior to rejoining the Groove this year.

"I want another shot at the NBA," Myers said. "I could have made the team if I hadn't been hurt. But I'm glad Greenville brought me back. I had a lot of success here last season. We won the championship. It was a lot of fun."

Myers is averaging 7.8 points, 1.2 assists, 1.6 rebounds, and 1.2 steals a game. He would like to see the Groove make a strong move in the postseason.

"It's not easy trying to repeat," Myers said. "You have to be ready to play every game. Basically, we want to be on top of our game as we go into the last month of the season."

Ron Rollerson, a Temple product, has been coming off the bench for the Asheville Altitude, located in Asheville, North Carolina. Rollerson, a 6'10", 295-pound center, is averaging 4.8 points and 3.4 rebounds a game. Prior to joining the Altitude, he spent time in training camps for the Seattle SuperSonics and the Philadelphia 76ers.

"I learned a lot in both camps," Rollerson said. "I came in as a free agent. I didn't have a guaranteed contract. You have to work hard all the time. You want to try to impress the coaches. That's what I'm trying to do in Asheville. The NBDL has a lot of pro scouts at the games. We're on national television [ESPN2]. It's a good situation as far as exposure."

Nate Johnson, ex–Camden High and Louisville star, deserves plenty of recognition. Johnson, a 6'6", 215-pound guard/forward, has been playing extremely well for the Columbus Riverdragons, located in Columbus, Georgia. He leads the NBDL in scoring with a 19.4 average.

"I didn't expect to lead the league in scoring," Johnson said. "I was at the Sixers' training camp, but things didn't work out for me. I hope I can continue to play at this level. Maybe something good will happen down the road."

Greer Getting with the Groove

THE *PHILADELPHIA TRIBUNE*, FEBRUARY 28, 2003

Lynn Greer, Temple's prolific scorer, has returned from Greece to play professional basketball for the Greenville Groove of the National Basketball Development League. The NBDL is a pro league sponsored by the NBA. The team is based in Greenville, South Carolina.

Greer, a 6'2" guard, spent the past seven months playing for the Near East team in Greece. He averaged 18 points a game during his stay in Europe. The former Engineering and Science standout believes the NBDL will provide him with a good opportunity to some day play in the NBA.

"This is going to be a new experience for me," Greer said. "I'm looking forward to it. I've only seen about two games. But the league is very competitive. It should be good for me. This move will take me closer to where I want to be.

"I thought playing over in Greece was nice. It was another experience for me. It was a different kind of basketball. They had good competition over there. I think it helped my game. It's something that if I had to, I would do it again."

Greer will join his former college teammate Kevin Lyde, who also plays for the Groove. In fact it was Lyde who told Tree Rollins, the former NBA star who coaches the Groove, about Greer.

"Kevin told his coach about me," Greer said. "I was home at the time. I'm really excited about playing with him again. I also talked to Ron [Rollerson, former Temple teammate], who plays in the league as well [with the Asheville Altitude]. They both had good things to say about the NBDL."

Greer finished his college career with 2,099 points. He's the Owls' second all-time leading scorer. He averaged 23.2 points a game in his senior year.

Although Greer can really shoot the basketball, he believes his position at the next level should be point guard. During his Temple career, he played the shooting and lead guard positions.

"I have to play point guard in the NBA," Greer said. "That's my position. I've learned a lot about playing there from coach [John] Chaney, Pepe Sanchez, Nate Blackwell, and Rick Brunson during the summertime. I've had nothing but great guys who taught me how to play the point guard position."

The NBDL games are televised on ESPN2. Greer will have a chance to play on national television.

"It will be nice for my family and friends to see me play," Greer said. "The NBDL gives you a lot of exposure. This is a good situation for me. It should really help me down the road."

Index

NAIA All-American, 2, 25, 105
NAIA Tournament Most
Valuable Player, 3
National Basketball Association
(NBA)
All-Rookie First Team, 79
All-Star Weekend, 79
draft picks, McKie and Jones as
first-round, 71–77
Most Valuable Player Award,
21
Philadelphia 76ers in 2001
NBA Finals, 19
Sixth Man Award, 19
Sportsmanship Award, 22
steal-to-turnover ratio, NBA's
best, 80
Temple players in the, 2, 71
National Basketball Development
League (NBDL), 175–77,
179–80
National Center for Fair and
Open Testing, 40, 41
National Collegiate Athletic
Association (NCAA), 89
Division II Tournaments, 4
Proposition 16, 40
Propositions 48 and 42, 14, 19,
20, 39–45, 104, 105, 137,
172
See also NCAA Tournament
National Division II Coach of the
Year, 11
National Invitation Tournament
(NIT), 7, 50, 65
NCAA Tournament
Final Eight, 47, 55
Final Four, 47
Owls appearances, 2, 7, 47, 48,
49–50, 63–64, 81, 89
Owls competitive playing
schedule, 10
Owls first victory in, 6
New Jersey Nets, 65, 126
New York Times, 41

Nightline, 41
Nike All-American Camp, 31
Norman, Jay, 88
North Carolina A&T State
University, 5, 6
Notre Dame University, 32

Ohio State University, 125
Orlando Magic, 20
Overton, Doug, 30
Owens, Chris, 144
Owens, Geoff, 166
Owls, the. *See* Temple University
Owls basketball team

Packer, Billy, 50
Penn, James "Scoonie," 125
Pennsylvania State University, 144
Perry, Tim, 2, 71, 95
Philadelphia Public School
System, 11
Philadelphia 76ers, 5, 9, 19, 21,
22, 65, 87, 165, 177
Phillips, Bill, 140
Pinnie, Dr. Anthony, 17
Pollak, Bill, 114
Pollard, Ernest, 39, 104
Poole, Leonard, 3–4, 169–70
Portland Trail Blazers, 19
McKie as first-round draft
pick, 71
McKie's rookie year with, 79,
80–81, 82–84
professional basketball, in Europe,
165–67
Proposition 16, 40
Proposition 42, 14, 19, 20, 40
Proposition 48, 14, 39–45, 104,
105, 137, 172
Public League (Philadelphia), 29,
31, 117, 119, 124, 148, 165,
171
Public League Player of the
Year, 2, 25, 31, 104, 123